Canadian Daily Language Activities

— Grade 7 —

Written by Eleanor M. Summers

Our Canadian Daily Language Activities series provides short and quick opportunities for students to review and reinforce skills in punctuation, grammar, spelling, language and reading comprehension. The Bonus Activities that follow each week of skills are fun tasks such as word and vocabulary puzzles, figurative language and reading exercises. A short interesting fact about Canada is the finishing touch!

ELEANOR M. SUMMERS is a retired teacher who is still actively involved in education. She has created many resources in language, science and history. As a writer, she enjoys creating practical and thought-provoking resources for teachers and parents.

Copyright © On The Mark Press 2016

This publication may be reproduced under licence from Access Copyright, or with the express written permission of On The Mark Press, or as permitted by law. All rights are otherwise reserved, and no part of this publication may be reproduced, stored in a retrieval system, or transmitted in any form or by any means, electronic, mechanical, photocopying, scanning, recording or otherwise, except as specifically authorized.

All Rights Reserved.
Printed in Canada.

Published in Canada by:
On The Mark Press
15 Dairy Avenue, Napanee, Ontario, K7R 1M4
www.onthemarkpress.com

#OTM2150

Topics cover:
Structural Form and Function, Heat and Temperature, Chemistry of Pure Substances and Mixtures.

#OTM2158

Topics cover:
The Planet Earth, Earth's Crust & Resources, and Heat in the Environment.

MASTER THE FACTS HISTORY SERIES

Master the Facts is a Hi/Lo Series developed to make history accessible to students at multiple skill levels and with various learning styles. Content is presented in a clear, concise manner for struggling learners with inquiry and application activities for students reading at grade level. There are two levels of questions for each topic. Illustrations, maps and diagrams visually enhance each topic and provide support for visual learners. 48 Master the Facts game cards review content learned.

#J197

#J198

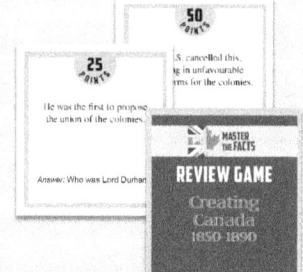

Teacher Notes

HOW TO USE: CANADIAN DAILY LANGUAGE ACTIVITIES

This book is divided into 32 weekly sections.

Each weekly section provides daily skill review and assessment activities.

ACTIVITIES 1 – 4

Focus is on:

- punctuation, capitalization, grammar, and spelling
- language and reading comprehension skills

ACTIVITY 5

Focus is on:

- a single language or reading skill

BONUS ACTIVITY

Provides opportunities for extended activities.

- word puzzles, vocabulary development
- spelling
- reading skills
- includes a short, interesting fact about Canada

STUDENT PROGRESS CHART

- Students record their daily score for each Language Activity.
- At the end of the week, they calculate their Total Score
- At the end of four weeks, students evaluate their performance.
- Students will require one copy of page 3 and three copies of page 4 to record results for entire 32 weeks. Teachers may wish to make back-to-back copies.

TEACHER SUGGESTIONS

- All activities may be completed for each week or teachers may exclude some.
- New skills may be completed as a whole class activity.
- Bonus Activities may be used at teachers' discretion.
- Correcting student work together will help model the correct responses.
- Monitor student mastery of skills from information on the Student Progress Chart.

_____ 'S PROGRESS CHART

How many did you get correct each day? Record your score on the chart.

Week	Activity 1	Activity 2	Activity 3	Activity 4	Activity 5	Total Score
#	/5	/5	/5	/5	/5	/25

Week	Activity 1	Activity 2	Activity 3	Activity 4	Activity 5	Total Score
#	/5	/5	/5	/5	/5	/25

Week	Activity 1	Activity 2	Activity 3	Activity 4	Activity 5	Total Score
#	/5	/5	/5	/5	/5	/25

Week	Activity 1	Activity 2	Activity 3	Activity 4	Activity 5	Total Score
#	/5	/5	/5	/5	/5	/25

My strongest skills are _____

My skills that need improvement are _____

The Bonus Activities I liked best are _____

Week	Activity 1	Activity 2	Activity 3	Activity 4	Activity 5	Total Score
#	/5	/5	/5	/5	/5	/25

Week	Activity 1	Activity 2	Activity 3	Activity 4	Activity 5	Total Score
#	/5	/5	/5	/5	/5	/25

Week	Activity 1	Activity 2	Activity 3	Activity 4	Activity 5	Total Score
#	/5	/5	/5	/5	/5	/25

Week	Activity 1	Activity 2	Activity 3	Activity 4	Activity 5	Total Score
#	/5	/5	/5	/5	/5	/25

My strongest skills are _____

My skills that need improvement are _____

The Bonus Activities I liked best are _____

_____ 'S PROGRESS CHART

How many did you get correct each day? Record your score on the chart.

Week	Activity 1	Activity 2	Activity 3	Activity 4	Activity 5	Total Score
#	/5	/5	/5	/5	/5	/25

Week	Activity 1	Activity 2	Activity 3	Activity 4	Activity 5	Total Score
#	/5	/5	/5	/5	/5	/25

Week	Activity 1	Activity 2	Activity 3	Activity 4	Activity 5	Total Score
#	/5	/5	/5	/5	/5	/25

Week	Activity 1	Activity 2	Activity 3	Activity 4	Activity 5	Total Score
#	/5	/5	/5	/5	/5	/25

My strongest skills are _____

My skills that need improvement are _____

The Bonus Activities I liked best are _____

Week	Activity 1	Activity 2	Activity 3	Activity 4	Activity 5	Total Score
#	/5	/5	/5	/5	/5	/25

Week	Activity 1	Activity 2	Activity 3	Activity 4	Activity 5	Total Score
#	/5	/5	/5	/5	/5	/25

Week	Activity 1	Activity 2	Activity 3	Activity 4	Activity 5	Total Score
#	/5	/5	/5	/5	/5	/25

Week	Activity 1	Activity 2	Activity 3	Activity 4	Activity 5	Total Score
#	/5	/5	/5	/5	/5	/25

My strongest skills are _____

My skills that need improvement are _____

The Bonus Activities I liked best are _____

DAILY LANGUAGE ACTIVITIES SKILLS LIST

This book provides many opportunities for practice of the following skills:

Vocabulary & Word Skills

- word meaning from context
- root words/prefixes/suffixes
- spelling
- syllabication
- synonyms/antonyms/homonyms
- contractions

Capitalization

- beginning of sentences
- proper names/titles of people
- names of places
- titles of books, songs, poems
- names of days, months, holidays
- abbreviations

Punctuation

- punctuation at the end of a sentence
- commas in a series
- commas in dates and addresses
- commas in compound and complex sentences
- commas after an introductory phrase/clause
- commas in direct address/parenthetical expressions
- commas after appositives
- commas between adjectives
- periods in abbreviations/initials
- punctuation & capitalization in simple dialogue
- use of colons & semicolons
- quotation marks in speech
- quotation marks: poems, songs, stories
- apostrophes in contractions
- apostrophes in possessives
- interjections
- punctuation in a friendly letter & business letters
- run on sentences
- underlining: books, plays, poems, magazines

Grammar & Word Usage

- pronouns: subject/object, possessive
- pronoun antecedent
- singular/plural nouns
- possessive nouns
- verb tenses
- verb types
- verb parts
- active & passive voice
- double negatives
- types of adjectives and adverbs
- correct form of adjective and adverbs
- correct article/determiner/adjective/adverb
- comparative/superlative forms
- subject/predicate
- subject – verb agreement
- conjunctions
- phrases & clauses
- sentence parts
- sentence types
- sentence structure
- sentence fragments
- sentence combinations

Reading Comprehension

- analogies
- figurative language
- inference
- idioms, proverbs

Reference Skills

- dictionary/thesaurus skills
- outlines
- summaries

Name: _____

WEEK 1

ACTIVITY 1

TOTAL /5

Correct these sentences.

1. donna said my faverite tv saterday show is dance club

   _____

2. i agree replied erica but i like austin and ally two

   _____

Rewrite this phrase using possessive nouns.

3. the jackets of Dan and Marty _____

Underline the verbs in this sentence.

4. Please stop at the store and buy some fruit. _____

Underline the *auxiliary* (helping) verb in this sentence.

5. Our school soccer team has won all their games this season.

Name: _____

WEEK 1

ACTIVITY 2

TOTAL /5

Write the best word to complete this sentence.

1. She _____ like that song on the radio.   **doesn't / wasn't / don't / isn't**

Correct these sentences.

2. gerry and tom asked jim too bring his knew glove to there basball pracktice

   _____

3. my parents is leaving tomorow four ther vacashion to new brunswick

   _____

Underline the direct object in each sentence.

4. Jack's mother made his favourite chocolate cake.

5. My little cousin asks a lot of silly questions.

Name: _____

Write the correct abbreviation for each word.

1. Highway _____

2. Royal Canadian Mounted Police _____

Correct these sentences.

3. lets have a movie partie with popcorn drinks icecream and candy

   _____

4. we could watch terror at the top and skare the girls

   _____

Underline the *object* of the preposition in this sentence.

5. We looked into the stream and saw tiny minnows.

WEEK 1
ACTIVITY 3
TOTAL /5

Name: _____

Circle the complete *subject* and underline the *complete predicate*.

1. Those boys practise every day for the cross-country race.

2. Determination and daily practice will help them to win.

Correct these sentences.

3. in 1535 jacques cartier saled up the st lawrence river on his weigh to quebec city

   _____

4. his guides pointed out the weigh to kanata or village and he gived the land this name

   _____

Circle the best auxiliary verbs to complete this sentence.

5. Jenna _____ reading the book Number the Stars.

   have been / is been / has been / is being

WEEK 1
ACTIVITY 4
TOTAL /5

Name: _____

Explain the meaning of the underlined expressions.

WEEK **1**

ACTIVITY **5**

TOTAL **/5**

1. <u>Buzz off!</u> I want to be alone.
   _____

2. I'm happy with my score. <u>Don't rain on my parade.</u>
   _____

3. Grandma says I am <u>the sunshine of her life.</u>
   _____

4. This job won't take me long to do. <u>It's a piece of cake!</u>
   _____

5. On my uncle's farm they <u>get up with the chickens.</u>
   _____

Name: _____

Bonus Activity: Cake Recipe Puzzle

WEEK **1**

Put the steps for this recipe in the correct order.

___ Pour batter into pan.

___ Preheat oven to 350°F

___ Remove cakes from pans. Cool completely before icing.

___ Grease sides and bottom of the pan.

___ Put cake mix, eggs, oil and water into a large bowl.

___ Bake for 35-40 minutes.

___ Stir ingredients together using a mixer or a whisk.

___ Use a toothpick to check to see if the cake is done. The toothpick will come out clean.

___ Let the cake cool in the pan for about 10 minutes.

___ Beat cake batter at medium speed for 2 minutes.

___ Carefully put the pans into the oven.

___ Enjoy your treat!

> In 1990, Paul Gallant of Montreal came up with a three-dimensional jigsaw puzzle at his kitchen table. In 1999, sales passed 30 million puzzles. His company continues to invent new puzzles and ship them worldwide.
> **MY CANADA**

Name: _____

WEEK 2

ACTIVITY 1

TOTAL /5

Correct these sentences.

1. jill recieved a A+ on her project called famous canadian authers

   _____

2. i done my projeckt on the canadian invenshun the canadarm

   _____

Write the plural form of each noun.

3. ax   _____

4. shelf   _____

Circle the *subject* and underline the *predicate*.

5. My cousins, Ella and Emma, take tennis lessons every Saturday.

Name: _____

WEEK 2

ACTIVITY 2

TOTAL /5

Underline the *predicate adjectives* in this sentence.

1. The woods looked dark and dangerous.

Write the *prefixes* and *suffixes* for these words.

2. unthinkable   _____   _____

3. reclaimed   _____   _____

Correct these sentences.

4. so many beavers was killed dering the fir trade that thay was almost extinct by the 1800s

   _____

5. when beaver hats went out of stile the beaver poplation recovered

   _____

Name: _____

Underline the *direct objects* in this sentence.

1. Abby won a medal and some money at the art contest.

Correct these sentences.

2. my sister patricia who goes to queens university want to be a docter
_____

3. she wents to werk with familys in the canadian arctic if she cans
_____

Write the singular of each noun.

4. heroes   _____

5. children   _____

WEEK 2
ACTIVITY 3
TOTAL /5

Name: _____

Correct these sentences.

1. in the 1850s peeple in canada couldnt deside on wear to put hour capital city
_____

2. they asked queen victoria to deside and she piked ottawa ontario
_____

Tell if these nouns are *singular possessive* or *plural possessive*.

3. the robin's nest   _____

4. the students' notes   _____

Underline the *object* of the preposition in this sentence.

5. When you get home, hang your jacket in the closet.

WEEK 2
ACTIVITY 4
TOTAL /5

SSR1150   ISBN: 9782771587464 © On The Mark Press

Name: _____

Tell whether each sentence is *simple, compound* or *complex*.

WEEK 2

ACTIVITY 5

1. Saturday is my thirteenth birthday. _____

2. The barbeque was free and everyone enjoyed the food. _____

3. If you go to the store, please buy me a candy bar. _____

TOTAL /5

4. We have lived in this town all of our life. _____

5. If there is human-like life on other planets, scientists have yet to find it.
_____

Name: _____

Bonus Activity: Context Clues

WEEK 2

A context clue is a hint from a sentence that helps you to figure out words you don't know. **Read each sentence. Write a definition of each underlined word.**

1. My pet canary <u>warbles</u> happily in her cage all day long.

   Meaning: _____

2. The confusing instructions that came with our computer <u>perplexed</u> my dad.

   Meaning: _____

3. Although she tries to be <u>punctual</u>, she is almost always late.

   Meaning: _____

4. Don't miss our next game. It is <u>crucial</u> to our team standing.

   Meaning: _____

> Would you ski if you had to walk back up the slope every time you went down? *Alex Foster* of Sainte-Agathe-des-Monts, Quebec invented and installed the first tow rope in the world in 1930. Some skiers nicknamed his invention Foster`s Folly at the time. Today people are willing to pay a tow charge.
>
> **MY CANADA**

Name: _____

Correct these sentences.

1. its an honor to meat you mrs king said rachel

_____

2. thank you said mrs king i am enjoying my visit to yore towne

_____

Underline the *subject* of these sentences.

3. Deep inside the cave, the hunter found the bear cub.

4. It was cold, hungry and lost.

Tell if this sentence is *simple, compound* or *complex*.

5. The mother bear will be searching everywhere and calling for her baby.

_____

WEEK 3
ACTIVITY 1
TOTAL /5

Name: _____

Underline the *prepositional phrase* in each sentence.

1. This beautiful bracelet was a gift from my favourite aunt.

2. She bought it while she was travelling in British Columbia.

Correct these sentences.

3. well you be abel to meat me at 300 pm at the movie theater asked harry

_____

4. i will bye hour snacks do you want popcorn and a drunk

_____

Underline the *independent clause* in this sentence.

5. Before I start my homework, I always get a snack to eat.

WEEK 3
ACTIVITY 2
TOTAL /5

Name: _____

WEEK 3 — ACTIVITY 3 — TOTAL /5

Underline the *independent clauses* in these sentences.

1. I like the new student even though I don't know him very well.

2. Whenever you have time, I would like a copy of that recipe.

Correct these sentences.

3. mr downes the musick teacher called a band pracktise for after school tonite

_____

4. bee on tyme and brang yore sheet musick fore hour new number

_____

Underline the *direct object* and circle the *indirect object* in this sentence.

5. I made cherry chip cupcakes for my niece's birthday.

Name: _____

WEEK 3 — ACTIVITY 4 — TOTAL /5

Underline the *subordinate clause* in each sentence.

1. If there is any ice cream in the freezer, we will have it for a treat.

2. If you go to bed too late, you will be tired in the morning.

Correct these sentences.

3. my cousins name is timothy james but i call him tj for short

_____

4. he were born on august 21 2000 in edmonton alberta

_____

Circle the *coordinating conjunctions* in this sentence.

5. I went to the mall and bought a new pair of cleats so I would be ready for the game.

Rewrite these sentences to punctuate the dialogue correctly.

1. Sandra muttered I'm never going to finish this report.
   _____

2. Get all of the ingredients together first Mom reminded me and then we will start to bake.
   _____

3. We will still play hard said Coach Drake even though some players are injured.
   _____

4. Just keep trying the voice inside my head whispered.
   _____

5. You never know what you can do said Dad until you are put to the test.
   _____

WEEK 3
ACTIVITY 5
TOTAL /5

Name: _____

Bonus Activity: Simile or Metaphor?

We use similes (like, as) and metaphors when we want to compare or describe things. **Tell whether the underlined expressions are a simile or a metaphor.**

1. When I tried to help Ray all he did was <u>bark at me</u>. _____

2. That music is so loud I feel <u>like I am at a rock concert</u>. _____

3. The breeze was <u>like a cool drink on a hot day</u>. _____

4. After a few days, my room was <u>a work of art</u>. _____

5. The ugly old chair was <u>as comfortable as a worn shoe</u>. _____

6. Grandma's blueberry pie tasted <u>like a slice of heaven</u>. _____

WEEK 3

MY CANADA

What is a STOL? A "short takeoff and landing" plane or bush plane. It was designed and built in 1947 by De Havilland Canada for bush pilots and the military. It made it possible to get people and cargoes in and out of remote parts of the North.

Name: _____

Correct these sentences.

WEEK 4

ACTIVITY 1

1. what shud we brang too the pot luck lunch on friday asked fred
   _____

2. scientists finded a rair fosill of a inseckt in northern manitoba
   _____

TOTAL /5

Tell the tense of the underlined verbs: *present, past* **or** *future*?

3. If I work hard, I <u>will pass</u> the test.   _____

4. Molly <u>bought</u> new boots for winter.   _____

Write the contraction for:

5. she is   _____

Name: _____

Underline the *predicate adjectives* **in this sentence.**

WEEK 4

1. The homemade fudge was sweet and gooey.

Tell if the sentence is *declarative, imperative, interrogative,* **or** *exclamatory*.

ACTIVITY 2

2. Get all of this mess cleaned up at once.   _____

Circle the *subject* **and underline the** *predicate* **in this sentence.**

TOTAL /5

3. The jet-black horses pulled the golden carriage.

Correct these sentences.

4. the furst version of o canada was wrote in french and performed in quebec city in 1880
   _____

5. o canada was named canada's offishul national anthem in 1980
   _____

Name: _____

Circle the *antecedent* of the underlined words.

1. The cat jumped down and landed on <u>its</u> feet.

2. Jimmy took off <u>his</u> socks and shoes and waded into the water.

Correct these sentences.

3. jenny jackson our nest door neighbor are studying to be a nerse
   _____

4. she hops to get a job at toronto sick kids hospital
   _____

Write the root (base) word for:

5. undesirable   _____

WEEK 4
ACTIVITY 3
TOTAL /5

Name: _____

Tell if these verbs are *present*, *past* or *future*.

1. We are buying a new dog this weekend.   _____

2. Dad fenced in a new yard to keep it safe.   _____

Correct these sentences.

3. the furst chapter of white fang are verry exsiting
   _____

4. have you ever thinked of traveling to canada's north
   _____

Explain the meaning of the underlined figure of speech.

5. I finished the test <u>in the nick of time</u>.
   _____

WEEK 4
ACTIVITY 4
TOTAL /5

Name: _____

Combine the following sentences to make one good sentence.

1. Toronto is the biggest city in Canada. Ottawa is the capital city of Canada.

   _____

2. Mr. Quinn is our history teacher. He is an expert on Confederation.

   _____

3. I love pancakes for breakfast. I cover them with delicious maple syrup.

   _____

4. Have you ever been across the Confederation Bridge? It joins Nova Scotia and P.E.I.

   _____

5. A cross-country trip would be exciting. It would be educational too.

   _____

WEEK 4
ACTIVITY 5
TOTAL /5

Name: _____

Bonus Activity: Imagine This!

Find and circle these words that name Canadian inventions in the puzzle.

b	a	s	k	e	t	b	a	l	l	i	t	m	e	p	s	s	o	t
w	t	n	l	a	e	a	s	a	i	h	s	u	p	e	r	m	a	n
a	v	m	w	a	l	i	w	c	g	t	q	i	d	t	g	s	i	c
h	w	a	v	r	e	c	h	r	h	o	c	k	e	y	n	e	z	a
p	l	o	l	c	p	m	a	o	t	e	o	t	c	t	a	i	t	n
y	v	i	k	e	h	c	h	s	b	s	n	d	f	w	p	o	d	a
c	f	o	g	h	o	r	n	s	u	m	s	g	h	p	a	o	m	d
r	w	k	o	o	n	n	e	e	l	n	s	e	e	t	t	b	m	a
s	l	a	c	o	e	d	u	c	b	o	r	r	r	n	t	a	i	r
h	g	o	a	l	i	e	m	a	s	k	i	k	l	p	e	c	b	m

Superman   lacrosse
basketball foghorn
Canadarm   hockey
telephone   toque
goalie mask zipper
lightbulb   atv

WEEK 4

Imagine a huge bug twice as big as a house cat, covered by a flat hard shell. No longer living, this creature is the world's largest known complete trilobite fossil. Scientists discovered its remains near Churchill, Manitoba in 1998.

MY CANADA

Name: _____

Circle the *present participle* in this sentence.

WEEK 5
ACTIVITY 1
TOTAL /5

1. The number of soccer fans is growing in Canada.

Correct these sentences.

2. wear does you all want to go for hour vacashun this summer asked dad

_____

3. lets viset sum interesting places rite around hear suggested mom

_____

Give the *possessive pronoun* for each one.

4. the backpacks of the boys   _____

5. the poodle of Callie   _____

Name: _____

Underline the *independent clause* in each sentence.

WEEK 5
ACTIVITY 2
TOTAL /5

1. You pick a movie to watch while I make the popcorn.

2. Even though I don't like scary movies, I will watch one with you.

Correct these sentences.

3. them womens done all the cooking for the fairfield annual turkey supper

_____

4. for desert they made pie blueberry charry punkin appel lemin and coconut creem

_____

_____

Is the underlined part a complete sentence or a fragment?

5. <u>With a big smile on her face.</u> Marlene accepted her prize. _____

Name: _____

WEEK 5 — ACTIVITY 3 — TOTAL /5

Underline the *subordinating conjunction* in each sentence.

1. I will call you as soon as I get home.

2. I'm going to the movies but I won't be late.

Circle the *simple subject* in this sentence.

3. Big cities often have many tall buildings.

Correct these sentences.

4. the ferst part of discovery north were filmed in hudson bay
   _____

5. allmost everybody on the film crue were frum the arctic or northern ontario
   _____

Name: _____

WEEK 5 — ACTIVITY 4 — TOTAL /5

Write the meaning of this idiom.

1. <u>Quick as a flash</u>, the chipmunk was gone. _____

Correct these sentences.

2. ant sue my dads sister is a nurse in medicine hat alberta
   _____

3. she trys to viset hour family each year at christmas and thanksgiving
   _____

Are these nouns *singular* or *plural*?

4. radios   _____

5. cloud   _____

Name: _____

Rewrite these sentences to correctly punctuate the dialogue in each sentence.

WEEK 5
ACTIVITY 5
TOTAL /5

1. Come in said Grandma I have made your favourite lunch
   _____

2. I have brought you a surprise from Mom I said Can you guess what it is
   _____

3. She is full of surprises said Grandma but I have an idea what it is
   _____

4. Let's wait until after lunch to open it okay I teased
   _____

5. Just how hungry are you Grandma teased me right back
   _____

Name: _____

WEEK 5

Bonus Activity: Concrete or Abstract?

A *concrete noun* is something you can see, hear, touch, smell or taste. An *abstract noun* is something you may not be able to see – an idea, a feeling, or a quality – but you know that it exists. **Read the story below. Circle the *concrete nouns in red* and the *abstract nouns in blue.***

Dad told Sam that today he was going to learn to ride his new bike. As Sam put his hands on the handlebars, Dad could see the fear on his face. Then Sam began to cry and big tears rolled down his cheeks. Dad held the bike as Sam pushed on the pedals. His balance was good and the bike started to move. Sam's concentration was paying off. Even his fear was going away. Suddenly, Dad let go without saying a word to Sam. Sam was riding all by himself. He didn't pick up much speed but he rode down the lane without any help. When Sam reached the end of the lane, he stopped and turned to his dad. With a big smile on his face, he yelled, "I did it!" Dad saw the pride on Sam's face. "Let's go tell your mother all about your accomplishment," he said.

> The oldest person to ski to the North Pole is Jack Mackenzie of Stittsville, Quebec. In 1999, he made the 100 kilometre trip from his base camp to the Pole in less than six days. He was 77 years old!   **MY CANADA**

Name: _____

Correct these sentences.

1. henry spended the hole day at the beech with uncle brad from vancouver
   _____

2. thay played frisbee toss made a hug sand castel and swum for ours
   _____

Circle the *direct object* and underline the *indirect object* in each sentence.

3. Sally writes short funny stories for children's magazines.

4. She donates her fees to the Save the Children Fund.

Rewrite this phrase using a possessive pronoun.

5. the horses belonging to Crossbar Ranch
   _____

WEEK 6
ACTIVITY 1
TOTAL /5

Name: _____

How many syllables does each word have?

1. celebration _____   magnificent _____

What is the tense of the underlined verbs?

2. Do you think that baby fox will survive? _____

3. The mother has fed it and kept it warm. _____

Correct these sentences.

4. pete road hims bike more faster than he had ever road befor
   _____

5. until he fells of he will ride more faster and more faster
   _____

WEEK 6
ACTIVITY 2
TOTAL /5

Name: _____

WEEK 6 — ACTIVITY 3 — TOTAL /5

Write the meaning of the underlined idiom.

1. My little brother really likes to sing but he <u>can't even carry a tune</u>.

_____

Underline the *subordinating conjunction* in each sentence.

2. Unless you finish your chores, you won't be going to the movies.

3. We will wait on the corner until you get there.

Correct these sentences.

4. arctic wolfs which live in canada's north pray on caribou

_____

5. thay traval in packs chase there pray suround them and then attack

_____

Name: _____

WEEK 6 — ACTIVITY 4 — TOTAL /5

Correct these sentences.

1. after you wash and dry the dishs put thum away on the shelfs in the cubboard

_____

2. dont brake eny or you will bee in big truble with grandma rose

_____

Circle the *subject* and underline the *predicate* in each sentence.

3. I haven't learned this new dance because it is very complicated.

4. I need a good partner to help me with the steps.

Circle the *subject* of this sentence.

5. Stop, look, and listen before crossing the street.   **we / they / you / her**

Name: _____

Rewrite this short paragraph, correcting all the punctuation errors.

Did you know that all living things in our oceans are endangered by pollution and who are the worst offenders thats right humans pollution can happen in many ways one way is the dumping of waste materials such as garbage and sewage right into the ocean an oil spill is another source of concern oil covers the gills of fish and causes them to smother birds get oil on their wings and are unable to fly do you know what happens when the birds try to clean oil off their wings often they get poisoned and die dont you agree that we should take steps to control pollution in our oceans

WEEK 6

ACTIVITY 5

TOTAL /5

_____
_____
_____
_____
_____
_____
_____

Name: _____

Bonus Activity: A Big "Con"

Complete each sentence with a "con" word from the Word Box. Use a dictionary if you need help with the meanings.

| convince   conscious   conservation   conclude   congested   consult |

WEEK 6

1. The mall was _____ with crazy shoppers looking for the best sales.

2. Did you _____ your parents to let you go to the party?

3. Please _____ your dentist if your tooth is still aching tonight.

4. Our _____ group hopes to plant 100 trees this Saturday.

5. Was he _____ after the accident?

6. This meeting will _____ by 8:00 pm.

> A Toronto chemist, John J. McLaughlin, invented *Canada Dry Ginger Ale*. He patented the secret recipe in 1907. Canada Dry products sell in 90 countries worldwide. It even is a suggested remedy for an upset stomach!

MY CANADA

Name: _____

WEEK 7
ACTIVITY 1
TOTAL /5

Correct these sentences.

1. moms dutch apple pye one ferst prize at farmersville fair in july
   _____

2. she developed this here speshail resipe it is a family secrit
   _____

Add a suffix to make these words into nouns.

3. advertise   _____

4. direct   _____

Underline the *direct object* and circle the *indirect object* in this sentence.

5. Our teacher told the class an exciting story about her trip to Australia.

Name: _____

WEEK 7
ACTIVITY 2
TOTAL /5

Complete sentence, or fragment?

1. In 1867, Canada   _____

2. Sir John A. Macdonald was our first Prime Minister. _____

Underline the *prepositional phrase* in this sentence.

3. We watched the comet streak across the night sky.

Correct these sentences.

4. susanna moodie comed to upper canada in 1832 from england
   _____

5. she wrote a book roughing it in the bush to told of the hard ships of pionear live
   _____

Name: _____

WEEK 7 — ACTIVITY 3

Write the correct abbreviation for:

1. Corporation _____

Correct these sentences.

2. little susie feeled vary proud wen her gots dressed all by herself
   _____

3. their is meny kinds of fish in troy lake but perch is the most commonest
   _____

Circle the *antecedent* for each underlined pronoun.

4. Some birds, like the ostrich, don't use their wings to fly.

5. Ms. Murray, my teacher, parks her car by the fence.

TOTAL /5

Name: _____

WEEK 7 — ACTIVITY 4

Correct these sentences.

1. ive bean lerning to down hill skee but i still fell down alot
   _____

2. my instruckter jake adams is won of the best at mt logan lodge
   _____

Complete this analogy.

3. Skin is to human as feathers are to _____.

Rewrite the phrase using a possessive pronoun.

4. the Olympic gold medals of Canada
   _____

5. the narrow streets of the old city
   _____

TOTAL /5

Name: _____

WEEK 7
ACTIVITY 5
TOTAL /5

Tell whether each sentence is *simple*, *compound*, or *complex*.

1. When I spotted my cousin, Mila, she was getting off the bus.
   _____

2. She was carrying some books and was wearing a backpack.
   _____

3. Mila is staying with my family for the whole summer.
   _____

4. Since we both love swimming, we will spend a lot of time at the beach.
   _____

5. We also plan to go hiking, do some shopping and go to the movies.
   _____

Name: _____

WEEK 7

Bonus Activity: Map It Out!

Read the following short story. Then, on the back of this page, create a *story map* that retells the story. Include details about the setting and the characters. Use speech balloons to add dialogue.

Sherry and Chad were walking home from school along their usual street. Chad spotted something over by a big maple tree. It was a brown leather purse. He picked it up and brought it over to show Sherry. They looked inside and saw an envelope with a great deal of cash. They looked through the purse and found a small red wallet. When they opened it up, they saw a card with the name "Mary Jenkins". They knew the owner. She was an elderly lady who lived alone not too far away. They looked at each other, nodded and headed for Mrs. Jenkins tiny white house.

MY CANADA

People all over the world play a famous game invented by two Canadians – Chris Haney and Scott Abbott. That game is *Trivial Pursuit*. There are more than a hundred separate editions of the game, in more than 30 countries. Have you ever played the electronic version?

Name: _____

WEEK 8 — ACTIVITY 1 — TOTAL /5

Correct these sentences.

1. emily howard stowe were the first women to practise medacine in canada
   _____

2. she faced meny hard ships but carryed on in her effert to help others
   _____

Circle the *direct object* and underline the *indirect object*.

3. Dad reads the daily newspaper each night.

4. We bought cotton candy at the fair.

Use a dictionary or a thesaurus to find a synonym for

5. special: _____

Name: _____

WEEK 8 — ACTIVITY 2 — TOTAL /5

Circle the *coordinating conjunction* in each sentence.

1. Read the instructions and follow them closely.

2. Dad tried but he was unable to fix my bike.

How many syllables in this word?

3. unfortunately _____

Correct these sentences.

4. my bother ben wakes up most early of all my family so he can ran befor school
   _____

5. he hops he can run in the annual jack ross marathon in september
   _____

Name: _____

Add a suffix to these words to make nouns.

1. navigate   _____

2. obligate   _____

Correct these sentences.

3. did you knew that the first settlrs in newfoundland was vikings
_____

4. yes i did replied allie i did a report called first visitors to north america
_____

Circle the *prepositions* in this sentence.

5. Our hike took us into the forest, through the trees, across a stream and into the field.

WEEK 8
ACTIVITY 3
TOTAL /5

Name: _____

Correct these sentences.

1. the play stranger after dark which were a student production were a grate success
_____

2. elli clarke played the heroine who resqued her best freind danny frum the stranger
_____

Circle the *antecedent* of the underlined pronoun.

3. Some people avoid going to the dentist because <u>they</u> are afraid.

Rewrite these words using a possessive noun.

4. the snow tires belonging to the van   _____

5. the math books belonging to Grade 7   _____

WEEK 8
ACTIVITY 4
TOTAL /5

Name: _____

Rewrite these sentences to correctly punctuate the dialogue.

1. Mom I'm sorry I'm so late Lily said sadly it won't happen again
   _____

2. Paul shouted last one in the pool is a rotten egg
   _____

3. Ouch yelled Tim you hit my hand with that hammer
   _____

4. Linda and I are going shopping in Montreal this weekend said Darcy
   _____

5. Have you ever read Storm Chaser asked William
   _____

WEEK 8
ACTIVITY 5
TOTAL /5

Name: _____

Bonus Activity: Words! Words! Words!

Fill in the blanks with a word (or words) that mean the same as the one in brackets. Use a dictionary or a thesaurus if you need help.

Mrs. Crawford always wears beautiful jewellery. She owns many _____ (*antique*) pieces. For everyday wear, she often chooses more _____ (*contemporary*) items. One day she _____ (*observed*) that some of her jewels had _____ (*strangely*) disappeared. She called the police and they agreed to _____ (*investigate*). After a short time, they had the _____ (*solution*). A crow had carried them off to its nest in a nearby tree!

WEEK 8

MY CANADA

Are you a fan of the really big picture? Then you would enjoy watching something on the IMAX screen. The first permanent IMAX theatre opened at Ontario Place in 1970. In 1990, the OMNIMAX system was created so you can seem to be a part of the action and visit places we may never go.

Name: _____

WEEK 9

ACTIVITY 1

TOTAL /5

Are these sentences *simple*, *compound*, or *complex*?

1. Jon has a crazy cat named Spotted Dog. _____

2. I love vanilla ice cream but I like chocolate better. _____

Correct these sentences.

3. seventy five millon years ago forests and warm sees covered most of canada
   _____

4. huge dinisaurs romed the earth lookin for food and water
   _____

Circle the *simple subject* and underline the *simple predicate*.

5. Little Mia dresses up as a princess every chance she gets.

Name: _____

WEEK 9

ACTIVITY 2

TOTAL /5

Circle the *conjunction* in each sentence.

1. She can't go out because she has to study for a history test.

2. As long as I have known her, school work comes first.

Write the plural of each noun.

3. frogman _____   reef _____

Correct these sentences.

4. i ware sunglases all yeer long becuz the son herts my eyes
   _____

5. insted of bying a house thay is gonna live in a apartment
   _____

WEEK 9 — ACTIVITY 3 — TOTAL /5

Is the underlined verb *transitive* or *intransitive*?

1. We <u>loaded</u> the wagon with wood from the big pile. _____

Correct these sentences.

2. wen the contestents give they're speach they well all set on the stage
   _____

3. only the ferst plase winner well go on to the nest leval said ms franklin
   _____

Write the correct abbreviation for:

4. October   _____

5. Canadian Broadcasting System   _____

WEEK 9 — ACTIVITY 4 — TOTAL /5

Correct these sentences.

1. david dont take none of those cookys or their wont be enuf for lunch
   _____

2. janice were born in cranbrook british columbia but now she lives in truro nova scotia
   _____

Use context clues to explain the meaning of the underlined word sentence.

3. Mom made a great <u>casserole</u> with macaroni, hamburg, spaghetti sauce and cheese.
   _____

Circle the antecedent of the underlined word.

4. The sunshine spread <u>its</u> warmth over my garden.

5. Hallie worked hard to win <u>her</u> award in swimming.

Name: _____

Combine the following sentences to make one good sentence.

WEEK **9**

ACTIVITY **5**

TOTAL **/5**

1. You will want dessert. You must eat your dinner first. You must drink your milk.
   _____

2. Mr. Ducharme is Keira's grandfather. He lives in Quebec. He visits her often.
   _____

3. Some dogs are great watchdogs. My dog is Digger. He just sleeps all day.
   _____

4. Mom makes chocolate chip cookies. They are the best. She uses Grandma's recipe.
   _____

5. Little Tommy was looking out the window. He was frowning. It was raining outside.
   _____

Name: _____

Bonus Activity: Oh, Land!

WEEK **9**

Colour the squares the correct colours.

Colour the **land formation words** red. Colour the **water words** blue. Colour the **"under the earth" words** green.

plateau	aluminum	iron	gulf
nickel	prairie	strait	diamond
gold	channel	muskeg	uranium
rapids	natural gas	oil	canyon

MY CANADA

Ice worms are very small worms that live on glaciers on the slopes of the Rocky Mountains. Their food is pollen and algae that they find there. If the temperature reaches around 5° Celsius, they can actually melt and die.

Name: _____

Are the following complete sentences, or fragments?

1. Ted hit the ball as hard as he could. _____

2. raced around the bases at top speed _____

Correct these sentences.

3. there phone ringed more louder then most phones due
   _____

4. eat your lunch said mrs bell and then you may go outside
   _____

Write the plural form of these words.

5. tornado _____   ferry _____

WEEK 10
ACTIVITY 1
TOTAL /5

Name: _____

Circle the *linking verb* in each sentence.

1. Sometimes I appear not to be listening, but I am.

2. This food smells so good that it is making me hungry.

Underline the *objects* of the prepositions in this sentence.

3. I dream of the day when I might travel on an airplane to Scotland.

Correct these sentences.

4. emily murphy writtted poplar books about erly life in canada
   _____

5. insted of using her own name she used the pin name janey canuck
   _____

WEEK 10
ACTIVITY 2
TOTAL /5

Name: _____

Add a suffix to this word to make an adverb.

1. fierce _____

Correct these sentences.

2. for this here resipe im gonna use butter milk brown suger and too eggs
_____

3. heet the oven to 350° use a glass pan and bake fore at leest 35 minits
_____

Tell if each sentence is *declarative, imperative, interrogative,* or *exclamatory*.

4. Wow! You did great in the race! _____

5. Don't forget to bring your books to my house. _____

WEEK 10
ACTIVITY 3
TOTAL /5

Name: _____

Rewrite these sentences to correct the run-ons.

1. I cannot eat peanut butter, I'm allergic to all nuts, I have to be very careful.
_____

2. Some foods have hidden nuts, cookies and cupcakes sometimes have nuts.
_____

Correct these sentences.

3. quebec city is famous for bonhomme and winter carnivel
_____

4. the st lawrence river forms a boundery between canada and the united states
_____

Write a good sentence to show the meaning of the word "delegate".

5. _____

WEEK 10
ACTIVITY 4
TOTAL /5

Name: _____

A *restrictive clause* is a clause that is **necessary** to the meaning of a sentence. A *non-restrictive clause* is a clause that is **not necessary** to the meaning. A non-restrictive clause is set off from the rest of the sentence by commas.

Write R (restrictive) or NR (non-restrictive) for the underlined clauses. Add commas where needed.

1. Students <u>who work hard</u> will be successful on this test. _____
2. Kingston <u>where Marty was born</u> is becoming a large city. _____
3. Lyle and Lucy <u>who live next door</u> have jobs in Toronto. _____
4. The wind <u>which was strong and cold</u> gave the hikers frostbite. _____
5. Harry <u>who was very tired</u> kept running until he reached the finish line. _____

Name: _____

Bonus Activity: Idioms

Complete the puzzle using words that finish these common idioms.

Across:
1. He kicked the _____
2. Last but not _____
3. A pain in the _____
4. Long arm of the _____
5. Sly as a _____
6. _____ your horses
7. Don't lose your _____

Down:
1. Busy as a _____
2. Clear as _____
3. Foot the _____
4. Face the _____
5. Quick as a _____

MY CANADA

Lobster fishing off the east coast of Canada has been a tradition for over 150 years. Lobster is often sold as a luxury item in restaurants today. But 200 years ago, lobster was the food of the poor people and considered to be the meal for servants and the lower class.

Name: _____

Correct these sentences.

1. canada have too offishul languages french and englush

   _____

2. both languages are teached in meny schools threw out canada

   _____

Underline the *subordinate clause* **in each sentence.**

3. She doesn't lose her temper even when she is really tired.

4. I will help you with your history project if I have time.

Underline the *prepositional phrases.*

5. Go to Stewart St., turn to the left, follow all the signs and you will find the yard sale.

WEEK **11**

ACTIVITY **1**

TOTAL **/5**

Name: _____

Is the tense of each verb *simple, past,* **or** *present*?

1. Please pass the pitcher of milk to me.   _____

2. I drank two glasses of milk for breakfast.   _____

Correct these sentences.

3. in kims gardin she growed tomatos beens radishs and zuckhini

   _____

4. it is grate to bee abel to eat frash vegetabels all summer long

   _____

Write the meaning of this figure of speech.

5. Don't give me any of your lip!

   _____

WEEK **11**

ACTIVITY **2**

TOTAL **/5**

Name: _____

Correct these sentences.

1. each morning i start the dey with a cuppa cofee tee or hot chocolite
   _____

2. fore brekfast i like hot serial toest fruit or maybe scambled eggs
   _____

Circle the *subject* and underline the *predicate* in each sentence.

3. Papers and cans littered the yard and made it look messy.

4. Sarah and her sister closed their eyes and made a wish.

Use context to explain the meaning of the underlined word.

5. Since you are so <u>flexible</u>, I will help you on Saturday.
   _____

WEEK **11**
ACTIVITY **3**
TOTAL **/5**

Name: _____

Are these sentences *declarative, interrogative, imperative,* or *exclamatory*?

1. Canada is located in the Northern Hemisphere. _____

2. What time shall we meet Zack and Ryan? _____

Correct these sentences.

3. my yongest sister bella likes all kinds of ice creem accept for strawbarry
   _____

4. i need sum knew shoes sum cleets and a pare of black flatts
   _____

Is the underlined verb *transitive* or *intransitive*?

5. He screeched to a stop to avoid hitting the little boy. _____

WEEK **11**
ACTIVITY **4**
TOTAL **/5**

Name: _____

Rewrite the sentences to correct the run-ons.

WEEK 11
ACTIVITY 5
TOTAL /5

1. Studying leaves is fascinating there are so many different kinds.
   _____

2. Leaves come in different shades of green no two kinds are the same.
   _____

3. Leaves that grow in shade are often dark green leaves that grow in sunlight are lighter.
   _____

4. A leaf's shape is important we can tell a lot about a tree from its leaf's shape.
   _____

5. Some leaves have complex shapes these shapes let the wind blow them easily.
   _____

Name: _____

Bonus Activity: Spot the Error!

WEEK 11

Find the word in each row that is misspelled. Write it correctly on the line. *You may need a dictionary to help you.*

1. refund   remodel   decode   previw   _____
2. deposet   pace   deflate   pretend   _____
3. fiction   grieff   unsafe   revise   _____
4. transfer defend   truthful penlty   _____
5. month   friendly wrench   businiss _____
6. surgery   magnit   usually   decide   _____

> **MY CANADA** Rick Hansen's Man in Motion Tour around the world in 1985–87 set a record as the *world's longest wheelchair journey*. He wore out 94 pairs of gloves and 160 wheelchair tires on his journey… and he raised $20 million dollars for spinal cord injury research!

Name: _____

Write the correct abbreviation for this word.

1. Senator _____

Correct these sentences.

2. mr burtch told us to opin hour books to the pome a ballad of john silver by john masefield
   _____

3. it are the story of john silver leader of the pirite gang in the story treasure island
   _____

Underline the *complete subject* and circle the *complete predicate*.

4. Everyone in my family worked hard to clean up leaves and plant the garden.

5. All the fans in the stands cheered loudly for the home team.

WEEK 12
ACTIVITY 1
TOTAL /5

Name: _____

Correct these sentences.

1. wen we fly to edmonton hour dog scoots well be staying home at the paws inn
   _____

2. it is a pet hotell wear animils can stay well they're ouwners is away frum home
   _____

Circle the *predicate adjectives* in these sentences.

3. Dad's research work is challenging and rewarding.

4. You seem sad and lonely today.

Write the contractions for these words.

5. who is _____   were not _____

WEEK 12
ACTIVITY 2
TOTAL /5

Name: _____

Correct these sentences.

WEEK 12
ACTIVITY 3
TOTAL /5

1. my bother didnt have no idea how i were able to find hims hidding plase in the dark
   _____

2. dave and eddie said their watching the action movie the return of zorro tonite
   _____

Circle the *antecedent* of the underlined pronouns.

3. The art summer program offers <u>its</u> program to students of all ages.

4. Jenny will be showing <u>her</u> best landscapes in their show.

How many syllables does each word have?

5. signature _____   appropriate _____

Name: _____

Correct these sentences.

WEEK 12
ACTIVITY 4
TOTAL /5

1. neither barry nor george past there history test on the war of 1812
   _____

2. miss downes sayed they cud do a makeup test on friday after school
   _____

Are these sentences *declarative, imperative, interrogative,* or *exclamatory*?

3. Congratulations, Paul, you won! _____

4. Greenland is in the Northern Hemisphere. _____

Is the underlined verb transitive or intransitive?

5. He <u>slammed</u> the door as hard as he could. _____

Name: _____

Rewrite these sentences to correctly punctuate the dialogue.

WEEK 12

ACTIVITY 5

TOTAL /5

1. I saw it with my own eyes said Gerry a stretch limo on main street
   _____

2. I think you are kidding me about that I answered back quickly
   _____

3. Who would be coming into our town in a car like that asked bill a rock star
   _____

4. Maybe it's a scout for a major hockey team added Toby or a basketball team
   _____

5. Hey guys shouted Roger did you see the limo for my cousin's wedding
   _____

Name: _____

Bonus Activity: What Does It Mean?

WEEK 12

Circle the correct meaning for the underlined word.

1. If you <u>incriminate</u> someone, you ___ him.   a) condemn   b) implicate   c) suspect

2. If you <u>disburse</u> money, you ___ it.   a) steal   b) refuse   c) pay out

3. If you <u>libel</u> someone, you ___ him.   a) injure   b) attack   c) defame

4. If you <u>negate</u> a statement, you ___ it.   a) value   b) deny   c) endure

5. If you have an <u>option</u>, you have a ___ .   a) choice   b) decision   c) contract

6. If you <u>encroach</u> on something, you ___ it.   a) infringe on   b) decorate   c) refuse

7. If you <u>allege</u> a fact, you ___ it.   a) admit   b) declare   c) conceal

> The "coolest" hotel in North America is the Hôtel de Glace in Quebec. It is made out of 15,000 tons of snow and 500,000 tons of ice. It is built from scratch each year from a new and different design so the new one is never quite the same as any of those built before it.

MY CANADA

Name: _____

WEEK 13 — ACTIVITY 1 — TOTAL /5

Underline the *conjunction* in this sentence.

1. We have to finish our homework, whether we want to or not.

Correct these sentences.

2. moms homemaid soup are a delishus treet for lunch on eny day
_____

3. she puts lottsa vegtables, chiken and some spices in it
_____

Rewrite these phrases using a possessive noun.

4. the Rocky Mountains that are in British Columbia
_____

5. the ATV that belongs to the Browns _____

Name: _____

WEEK 13 — ACTIVITY 2 — TOTAL /5

Underline the *subordinate clause* in this sentence.

1. Because I missed the bus, I was late for class.

Write a *synonym* and a *antonym* for this word.

2. **fake** Synonym: _____ Antonym: _____

Correct these sentences.

3. tammy practises her skating evry day becuz she wants to win the competishun
_____

4. uncle steve colects old clocks he bys them at flee markets and yard sails
_____

Rewrite the phrase using a contraction.

5. Jenny does not _____

Name: _____

Write the *form of the adjective* to best complete this sentence.

1. Mom is the _____ (good) dancer in her family.

Correct these sentences.

2. there too dogs barked all nite and waked up the hole neighbor hood
   _____

3. we visited the canadian national exhibition or cne while we was in toronto
   _____

Add a suffix to these words to make nouns.

4. rough   _____

5. fight   _____

WEEK 13
ACTIVITY 3
TOTAL /5

Name: _____

Write a good sentence that shows the meaning for this word: pretext

1. _____

Correct these sentences.

2. todd mrs greenwood said pleas explane yore anser to the class
   _____

3. bye the time we reterned from fishing we was wet tried and hungary
   _____

Circle the subject of each sentence.

4. Nancy, take the cookies out of the oven.

5. Cookies don't take very long to cook.

WEEK 13
ACTIVITY 4
TOTAL /5

Name: _____

Combine the following sentences to make one good sentence.

WEEK 13
ACTIVITY 5
TOTAL /5

1. Prince Edward Island has a rocky coast. This may be dangerous for ships. Lighthouses warn ships of the dangers.

   _____

2. The Calgary Stampede is in July. It runs for ten days. One exciting event is chuck wagon racing.

   _____

3. Saskatchewan is a prairie province. It is famous for the wheat grown there. The land is very flat.

   _____

4. The Canadian side of Niagara Falls is in Ontario. It is called Horseshoe Falls. Many tourists like to visit there.

   _____

Name: _____

WEEK 13
BONUS ACTIVITY

Bonus Activity: Categories

Circle the word in each group that does not belong.

1. software	mouse	chain	program	flashdrive
2. dawn	daylight	sunrise	twilight	hyphen
3. cyclone	generator	typhoon	tornado	hurricane
4. almond	chocolate	butterscotch	vanilla	strawberry
5. proverb	pronoun	adjective	adverb	preposition
6. period	comma	apostrophe	colon	clause
7. mythology	petrology	geology	biology	zoology

MY CANADA

Barenaked Ladies are the first Canadian band to have a Ben & Jerry's ice cream treat named in their honour. "If I Had 1,000,000 Flavours" contains vanilla and chocolate ice cream, peanut butter cups, chocolate-covered toffee, white chocolate chunks and chocolate-covered almonds. YUM!!

Name: _____

Correct these sentences.

1. in 1967 canada holed a big celebrashun for it's first sentennial

   _____

2. in 2017 we will selebrate won hundred fiffty years as a nashun

   _____

Explain the meaning of the underlined word by using context clues.

3. Our teachers work hard to improve the <u>literacy</u> of their students.

   _____

Circle the *auxiliary (helping) verbs* in these sentences.

4. If your story is written, you may read it to me.

5. The whole event is becoming clearer to me now.

WEEK 14
ACTIVITY 1
TOTAL /5

Name: _____

Correct these sentences.

1. my cousin are named april louise it is her grandmothers name two

   _____

2. playing baskitball running cross-country and swiming is good excercise

   _____

Circle the best word to complete the sentence.

3. These earrings are my aunt's. They are _____ **theirs / ours / mine / hers**

4. They own all of that property. It is _____ **theirs / ours / mine / his**

Number these words on alphabetical order.

5. ___ lily   ___ link   ___ limp   ___ lime   ___ linen   ___ livid

WEEK 14
ACTIVITY 2
TOTAL /5

46   SSR1150   ISBN: 9782771587464 © On The Mark Press

Name: _____

WEEK 14 — ACTIVITY 3 — TOTAL /5

Underline the *past participles* in these sentences.

1. Before noon, we had caught ten fish for our fish fry.

2. He was running five kilometres a day to get in shape.

Correct these sentences.

3. great grandpa don turned 100 on october 10 we had a big party to sellebrate
   _____

4. sam our bassball teem captin trys hard to keep hour teem working there best
   _____

Circle the *simple subject* of this sentence.

5. An aide to the Prime Minister will arrange that meeting.

Name: _____

WEEK 14 — ACTIVITY 4 — TOTAL /5

Correct these sentences.

1. my moms favorit tv show is chopped she watches it every weak
   _____

2. wunce i asked her would you ever like to apper on that show
   _____

Circle the *antecedent* of the underlined pronouns.

3. The cat woke up, stretching <u>its</u> legs.

4. Selena's cousins said they would help <u>her</u> sew the costumes.

Add a prefix to this word to make an adjective.

5. acceptable _____

Name: _____

A *restrictive clause* is a clause that is **necessary** to the meaning of a sentence. A *non-restrictive clause* is a clause that is **not necessary** to the meaning. A non-restrictive clause is set off from the rest of the sentence by commas.

Write R (restrictive) or NR (non-restrictive) for the underlined clauses. Add commas where needed.

WEEK 14

ACTIVITY 5

TOTAL /5

1. Foods <u>that are high in sugar</u> are high in calories too. _____

2. Children <u>who disobey the rules</u> will lose their privileges. _____

3. Our cottage is on an island <u>where everyone knows each other</u>. _____

4. Chocolate <u>which is my favourite flavour</u> is a popular choice of ice cream. _____

5. Sherry <u>who is my best friend</u> won the Artist of the Year Award. _____

Name: _____

Bonus Activity: Analogies

Complete the following analogies.

WEEK 14

1. Salt is to pepper as bread is to _____

2. Author is to book as artist is to _____

3. Research is to researcher as garden is to _____

4. Breakfast is to lunch as morning is to _____

5. TV is to commercial as magazine is to _____

6. Manager is to store as principal is to _____

7. Chair is to table as mattress is to _____

Clara Hughes won medals in both the Summer and Winter Olympics. She won two bronzes for cycling (1996) and a gold, a silver, and two bronzes in speed skating across three Games (2002, 2006, 2010).

MY CANADA

Name: _____

WEEK 15
ACTIVITY 1
TOTAL /5

Are the underlined verbs *transitive* or *intransitive*?

1. Janet <u>made</u> pizza for us for dinner. _____

2. Andy <u>sneezed</u> loudly and scared the baby. _____

Circle the *prepositional phrases* in this sentence.

3. We drove to the beach and ate our lunch at the picnic table.

Correct these sentences.

4. becuz she am so quite she never desturbs enyone
   _____

5. help me sat the tabel called mom sew we can eat erly
   _____

Name: _____

WEEK 15
ACTIVITY 2
TOTAL /5

Underline the *complete subject* and circle the *simple subject*.

1. My friend, Sasha, is learning how to dive.

Correct these sentences.

2. please tell the waiter that we dont need eny more bred with hour meel
   _____

3. he cutted his foot on a clame shall at the beech it bleeded alot
   _____

Write the plural form of each noun.

4. formula _____

5. piano _____

SSR1150   ISBN: 9782771587464 © On The Mark Press

Name: _____

Circle the *linking verb* in this sentence.

1. Grandma's cookies and doughnuts tasted delicious.

Tell if each sentence is *declarative*, *imperative*, *interrogative*, or *exclamatory*.

2. Study tonight because the big test is tomorrow. _____

3. I need to get a good night's sleep before the test. _____

Correct these sentences.

4. sarahs note sadi meat me at the libary after scienc class

   _____

5. puffins next along the avalon coastline of newfoundland

   _____

WEEK 15
ACTIVITY 3
TOTAL /5

Name: _____

Write the correct abbreviation for each word.

1. kilogram   _____

2. centimetre   _____

Correct these sentences.

3. a ice road is a name gived to a river that freezes with ice over a metre thick

   _____

4. thay is used as roads dering the arctic winter they even hold heavy trucks

   _____

Underline the *present participle* in this sentence.

5. Jan owns a flourishing business.

WEEK 15
ACTIVITY 4
TOTAL /5

Name: _____

Combine the following sentences to make one good sentence.

1. We are going swimming. We are going to Crystal Beach. Some friends are going with us.
   _____

2. I like to read good books. I like the room to be quiet. I like to be all by myself when I read.
   _____

3. Where is my red sweater? It is brand new. I left in on the couch last night.
   _____

4. This is a gloomy day. It looks like it is going to rain. This would be a good day for a nap.
   _____

WEEK 15
ACTIVITY 5
TOTAL /5

Name: _____

Bonus Activity: Story Board

On the back, create a storyboard for the following short story. Illustrate each paragraph in one box on the storyboard. Use speech bubbles to retell the story.

1. Laurie and Chloe were friends and neighbours. They loved to solve mysteries so they began their own club. They used a small shed in Chloe's back yard as a clubhouse. The sign above the door said, " Mystery Solvers Club"

2. One Saturday afternoon, just before their meeting, Chloe went to her room to get her journal. It was missing! She looked everywhere but could not find it.

3. Chloe ran to the backyard to tell the others the bad news. "We will help you look for it," they said. They needed the club notes to solve a mystery that they were working on.

4. All of a sudden Chloe said, "Wait a minute. I think I know where to start to look."

WEEK 15

BONUS ACTIVITY

MY CANADA Edouard Arsenault was a lighthouse keeper at Cap-Egmont, P.E.I., who liked to collect bottles. He decided to start building with them. Between 1980 and 1984, he cemented together 25,000 bottles to build three fantasy houses. Today this is a tourist attraction.

Name: _____

Explain the meaning of the underlined figure of speech.

1. We were just walking around and <u>killing time</u>.

   _____

Underline the *subordinate clause* in each sentence.

2. If you arrive early at the party, you can help me set up the tables.

3. When the guest of honour gets here, we will all yell, "Surprise!"

Correct these sentences.

4. if you eats more quicker then others you mite get a stomack ack

   _____

5. wen mr howard dropped hims briefcase all hims papers blue away

   _____

WEEK 16
ACTIVITY 1
TOTAL /5

Name: _____

Circle the *subordinating conjunction* in this sentence.

1. We won't ask him to help us unless we really need him.

Are the underlined verbs *transitive* or *intransitive*?

2. We elected a new class president.   _____

3. We are leaving home at exactly 8:00 am for the train station.

   _____

Correct these sentences.

4. whenever your worryed about sumthing remember to breath deep

   _____

5. charlotte who is my cousen is takeing a cake decerating class at parkwood high

   _____

WEEK 16
ACTIVITY 2
TOTAL /5

Name: _____

Add a suffix to these words to make adjectives.

1. truth   _____

2. worth   _____

Circle the *correlative conjunctions* in this sentence.

3. The soccer team will play their game whether it rains or not.

Correct these sentences.

4. yesterday we find sum glasses a jacket and a libary book on the park bench
   _____

5. we dont no who's they are we left them at the publik libary
   _____

WEEK 16
ACTIVITY 3
TOTAL /5

Name: _____

Correct these sentences.

1. wood you like toest serial or scambled aggs for brekfest asked mom
   _____

2. how about a bacin lettuse and tomatoe sandwitch i replied
   _____

Underline the *subject* and circle the *predicate* in each sentence.

3. The winning soccer team and their coach were congratulated after the game.

4. We will check tomorrow's newspaper for their picture.

How many syllables in each word?

5. hallucination _____   prosperous _____

WEEK 16
ACTIVITY 4
TOTAL /5

Name: _____

Rewrite this short paragraph, correcting all the punctuation errors.

When the first settlers came to Canada they had to find shelter quickly their first homes were log cabins huts made from mud and bark or dugouts which were simply caves dug into hillsides can you imagine surviving in such harsh conditions as soon as possible the settlers worked to replace these temporary homes with more safe comfortable ones most homes were made of wood some had wooden shingles but most homes had thatched roofs

WEEK 16
ACTIVITY 5
TOTAL /5

_____
_____
_____
_____
_____
_____

Name: _____

Bonus Activity: Strange Names Word Search

Here are some strange place names in Canada. Find and circle the words written in capital letters.

WEEK 16

BROKEN SKULL River
BONE Brook   KIDNEY Bay
BUTT Lake   Lac TOE
CHEST Island   Moose JAW
ELBOW   NAIL Pond
EYEBROW   NOGGIN Cove
FINGER Mt.   THUMB Island
FOOT Cape   TOOTH Ridge
HEART'S Delight

B	R	O	K	E	N	S	K	U	L	L	A	G	T	M
O	A	O	I	E	F	F	C	E	K	A	T	T	V	A
N	I	S	D	J	W	C	H	L	F	L	U	E	D	I
E	R	D	N	H	A	T	E	Y	E	B	R	O	W	R
A	E	H	E	A	R	T	S	L	I	Y	N	A	I	L
E	G	O	Y	F	O	O	T	N	B	E	C	N	C	O
A	N	L	D	T	H	O	E	F	N	O	G	G	I	N
S	I	C	R	E	E	T	E	O	T	I	W	A	J	O
L	F	I	V	E	T	H	U	M	B	I	L	Y	L	T

The first eight women's *World Hockey Championship* tournaments were won by Canada. Canada beat the American team in each championship game.

MY CANADA

54   SSR1150   ISBN: 9782771587464 © On The Mark Press

Name: _____

Correct these sentences.

1. billy trys to studdy more hard this hear year for his hisstory tests
   _____

2. he want to bee on the honer role wen him graduates in june
   _____

Rewrite these phrases using *possessive nouns*.

3. the most important export of Canada _____

4. the ingredients in chocolate cake _____

Circle the best words or words to complete this sentence.

5. Peter is the ___ boy I know.   **honestly / honester / honestest / most honest**

WEEK **17**
ACTIVITY **1**
TOTAL **/5**

Name: _____

Underline the *objects* **of the prepositions in these sentences.**

1. Over the hills, and through the woods, to grandmother's house, we go.
2. We spent the day at the beach, playing in the sand and jumping off the dock.

Correct these sentences.

3. rudy can you bye sum food for rover when you go shoping asked dale
   _____

4. what kinde is goodest for a dog of his sise replied rudy
   _____

Underline the simple subject and circle the *simple predicate*.

5. Waiting for their favourite runner to pass by, the fans cheered when she came into sight.

WEEK **17**
ACTIVITY **2**
TOTAL **/5**

Name: _____

WEEK 17

ACTIVITY 3

TOTAL /5

Underline the *conjunctions* in these sentences.

1. After we finished our homework, we watched TV.

2. Mom was mad because we left our rooms in a mess.

Write the contraction for this word.

3. should have _____

Correct these sentences.

4. rockwood high will play the finale game of the seeson aganst johnstown high
   _____

5. all dering the game the croud were very enthuceastic about the skore
   _____

Name: _____

WEEK 17

ACTIVITY 4

TOTAL /5

Write the correct abbreviation for each word.

1. Captain _____

2. April _____

Correct these sentences.

3. on july 1 1867 fore provinces united to becum the dominion of canada
   _____

4. ovur the next few years more provences joined and hour country growed in size
   _____

Complete the analogy.

5. meatball is to spaghetti as chocolate chip is to _____

Name: _____

Combine the following sentences to make one good sentence.

WEEK **17**

ACTIVITY **5**

TOTAL **/5**

1. Processed food contains a lot of salt. It is not a good idea to eat too much processed food.

   _____

2. Jan's family used to live in Calgary. They live in Edmonton now.

   _____

3. Deciduous trees lose their leaves every year. It is hard work to clean up all those leaves.

   _____

4. Our public library has great books. I borrow books from there all the time.

   _____

5. I have a new teacher this year. Her name is Ms. Doyle. She is a funny person.

   _____

Name: _____

Bonus Activity: Fix It!

This paragraph contains a number of spelling errors. Read the sentences. Underline the spelling mistakes. Write the correct spelling above each error.

WEEK **17**

    Marianne wanted to aquire a saltwater accquarum. She was worried about the expence and the care it wood need. So she did some reseach so she wood no the exxact care and time envolved. One sorce said she needed to put the water in the aquarium and wait six weeks before she added the fish. "Good greif! That's two mush work." thought Marianne. So she got a puppy from her nieghbour insted.

MY CANADA

People living on the north side of Canusa Avenue in Stanstead, Québec are Canadian while people living across the street are American and are residents of Derby Line, Vermont. When the American residents pull out of their driveway, they are really in Canada and must report to the border post.

Name: _____

Are the following texts a complete sentence, or a fragment?

1. Ian's sister Cindy and her friend Erica. _____

2. The girls like to go shopping together. _____

Correct these sentences.

3. we hasnt put away all of them there groceres so don't look in the cubboard
   _____

4. if you wants to help us we is glad to has won moore persin
   _____

Underline the helping, or *auxiliary*, verbs in this sentence.

5. Josie doesn't like getting cold so she will stay inside if the temperature is falling fast.

WEEK 18
ACTIVITY 1
TOTAL /5

Name: _____

Circle the *direct object* and underline the *indirect object*.

1. Mom hit the garage door with her car.

2. I will finish my homework on my laptop.

Correct these sentences.

3. set in the same seets wile i check yore atendunce said mr clark
   _____

4. terrifc he said this must be a record evrone is presant today
   _____

Circle the word with the most syllables.

5. commercial   domination   humiliate   organization

WEEK 18
ACTIVITY 2
TOTAL /5

Name: _____

WEEK 18

ACTIVITY 3

TOTAL /5

Correct these sentences.

1. becuase everone in my famly like annimals we has three cats too dogs and a rabit
   _____

2. everyone help to fed water and somtimes bathe each won of hour pets
   _____

Write the *root*, or base, word for each word.

3. disembark   _____

4. adjustment   _____

Underline the helping, or *auxiliary*, verb in this sentence.

5. If you need help, you should ask your teacher.

Name: _____

WEEK 18

ACTIVITY 4

TOTAL /5

Declarative, interrogative, imperative, or *exclamatory*?

1. What a great day for our baseball team! _____

Correct these sentences.

2. when the litle kids play in the sandbox there shoos gets full of durt
   _____

3. they has lottsa fun playing with there pales shovals and toy trucks
   _____

Circle the best word to complete these sentences.

4. Those books belong to Dan. They are _____.   **him / his / he / their**

5. The Jeffersons own that house. It is _____.   **their / they / theirs / them**

Name: _____

Rewrite these sentences to correctly punctuate the dialogue.

WEEK 18
ACTIVITY 5
TOTAL /5

1. A voice over the loudspeaker said would Jon Kent please come to the office
   _____

2. Who are the candidates for school mayor asked the principal.
   _____

3. Candidates need to prepare a speech said Mrs Owen They will speak on Friday
   _____

4. We need to work together said Roger if we are going to help Annie win
   _____

5. Whose slogan is Want the best vote for Tess
   _____

Name: _____

Bonus Activity: A Bunch of Groups

WEEK 18

Animals form groups to raise babies, hunt, play and to protect themselves. These animal groups have special names. **Match the animals to the correct group name.**

bears   lions   elephants   geese   ants   sheep   seals

1. a gaggle of _____   5. a drove of _____

2. a sloth of _____   6. a pod of _____

3. a herd of _____   7. a pride of _____

4. a colony of _____

MY CANADA Canada is pretty cool! Canada is just about the coolest country – literally. It competes with Russia for first place as *the coldest nation* in the world. The average daily annual temperature is -5.6°C.

Name: _____

Correct these sentences.

1. i seen a moose wen i were in newfoundland with my famly in july
   _____

2. it were wanderin down the rode it werent paying eny attenshun to the traffick
   _____

ACTIVITY 1

TOTAL /5

Underline the *object* of the preposition in this sentence.

3. George put his jacket in the closet.

Circle the best word to complete each sentence.

4. This van belongs to my family. It is _____   **my / ours / us / mine**

5. That cute kitten belongs to the Browns. It is _____   **them / their / theirs / his**

Name: _____

Rewrite this sentence to correct the run-on.

1. Here are three types of angles measure them in degrees.
   _____

Correct these sentences.

2. my cousen harry who live in windsor ontario dont has no brothers or sisters
   _____

ACTIVITY 2

TOTAL /5

3. he like to viset hour farm each sommer becuz we has a big famly
   _____

Underline the *subordinate clause* in each sentence.

4. You won't be allowed to go until your mother gives you permission.

5. After we go to the movie, we are going to Pizza Palace.

Name: _____

Underline the *linking verb* in each sentence.

1. We visited both the Parliament Buildings and the Royal Canadian Mint.

2. The weather is better today than yesterday.

3. It becomes better each day as summer approaches.

Correct these sentences.

4. in 1894 margaret mashall saunders writed beautiful joe autobiography of a dog
   _____

5. it are beleived to bee the ferst canadian book to cell won millon copys
   _____

ACTIVITY 3

TOTAL /

Name: _____

Are these sentences *declarative, interrogative, imperative,* or *exclamatory*?

1. Please put your things away before you leave the classroom.
   _____

2. Can you help me restart my computer?   _____

What is the meaning of the underlined expression?

3. When Mom heard that plan, she <u>nipped it in the bud</u>. _____

Correct these sentences.

4. we dont no who's backpack were founded on the bus
   _____

5. we leaved it in the lost and found nere the principals offace
   _____

ACTIVITY 4

TOTAL /

Name: _____

Write the numbers 1 – 21 to put these words in alphabetical order.

____ mysterious   ____ antique   ____ mansion

____ investigate   ____ contemporary   ____ reside

____ solution   ____ electric   ____ bungalow

____ scarlet   ____ genuine   ____ elegant

____ ivory   ____ sincere   ____ dowdy

____ indigo   ____ impostor   ____ wandering

____ accumulate   ____ acquire   ____ zany

ACTIVITY
5

TOTAL
/5

Name: _____

Bonus Activity: In Other Words

Our English language borrows words from other languages. **Match these French words with their meanings.**

1. antique ____   6. elite ____   a) strange   e) driver of a car

2. bizarre ____   7. garage ____   b) choice, select   f) a place to keep a car

3. chauffeur ____   8. valet ____   c) a personal servant   g) expert critic

4. cliche ____   d) overworked expression   h) very old, ancient

5. connoisseur ____

The *first known photograph of Canada* shows a picture of Niagara Falls. It was taken in 1840 by an English chemist who was visiting America. It also shows some buildings in Niagara Falls, including the Clifton Hotel which was one of the most elegant of its time.

Name: _____

Complete sentence fragment.

1. Stopping to look both ways, Kyle began to _____

Underline the correlative conjunction in each sentence.

2. Neither Will nor Wally knew the correct answer to my question.

3. We don't know for sure whether we leave at 7:00 a.m. or 7:30 a.m.

Correct these sentences.

4. because jen and me wasnt reddy for the test we scored worser then we shoodve
   _____

5. we is gonna ask ms kerr if we is abel to rewright it on monday
   _____

WEEK 20
ACTIVITY 1
TOTAL /5

Name: _____

Correct these sentences.

1. i needs to chang my close said mark befour i goes on a hick with youse
   _____

2. brang yore backpac with some snacs a water bottel and bug spray i yelled
   _____

Underline the *independent clause* in each sentence.

3. You are not going to make the team unless you come to practice each day.

4. While you pick up the toys, I will load the dishwasher.

Circle the subject of this sentence.

5. Clean off the table and we will play a board game.   **we / they / she / you**

WEEK 20
ACTIVITY 2
TOTAL /5

Name: _____

Underline the *subordinating conjunction* in this sentence.

1. I can't leave yet because my mother is not home from work.

Correct these sentences.

2. lets bye sum knew pensils crayens and notbooks fore sckool
   _____

3. thay gots big bargins on sckool supplys rite now at the best price and value store
   _____

Circle the *antecedent* of the underlined pronoun.

4. Squirrels like to build <u>their</u> nests high up in trees.

5. The osprey laid four eggs in <u>its</u> nest.

WEEK 20
ACTIVITY 3
TOTAL /5

Name: _____

Write the underlined words to include a contraction.

1. <u>We have not</u> seen that new movie yet.   _____

2. <u>It will</u> soon be in theatres near us.   _____

Correct these sentences.

3. queen elizabeth ll canadas queen are the longist raining monarch in are histery
   _____

4. her lives in buckinham palice in london england with hers husbind prince phillip
   _____

Underline the personified word in this sentence.

5. The sun smiled down on the earth below.

WEEK 20
ACTIVITY 4
TOTAL /5

SSR1150   ISBN: 9782771587464 © On The Mark Press

Name: _____

Combine the following sentences to make one good sentence.

1. I won't be able to meet you at noon. I have to get my hair cut. I will meet you later.
   _____

2. My dad likes to read the sports section of the newspaper. Mom likes the gardening news.
   _____

3. Peanuts are related to peas and beans. They grow underground. They are called legumes.
   _____

4. Dr. Greene is our dentist. She has a big practice. Her office is in Medford.
   _____

WEEK 20
ACTIVITY 5
TOTAL /5

Name: _____

Bonus Activity: Champlain in the Colonies

Choose a word or words from the word box that means the same as the underlined word.

| large tracts of land | craftsmen |
| peasants | rich settlers |

1. Champlain believed that his Habitation would grow large and <u>prosperous</u>.
   _____

2. <u>Artisans</u>, labourers and farmers arrived to live at Champlain's Habitation.
   _____

3. But, fifty years later, barely 3,000 <u>colonists</u> had survived to live in New France.
   _____

4. The land in New France was divided into sections called <u>seigneuries</u>.
   _____

WEEK 20

MY CANADA
Canada's largest rodent is the *beaver*. We're so proud of it, we put it on our nickel. The beaver received official status as a national emblem on March 24, 1975.

Name: _____

Circle the *antecedent* of the underlined pronoun.

1. The boys and girls were already in <u>their</u> seats.
   _____

2. If you spill chocolate milk on your shirt, <u>it</u> will leave a stain.
   _____

Correct these sentences.

3. that there farris weel tern fastest than eny ride i has ever bin on
   _____

4. as my aunt celia borded the bus for moose jaw i waved good by sadly
   _____

Circle the *coordinating conjunctions* in this sentence.

5. Emma and Drew love computer games, but Andy doesn't.

WEEK 21
ACTIVITY 1
TOTAL /5

Name: _____

Correct these sentences.

1. wood you like to life in paris rome or london in the futur
   _____

2. not me i wood perfer victoria quebec city or edmonton
   _____

Add a suffix to these words to make adjectives.

3. squiggle _____

4. accident _____

Is this sentence *simple*, *compound* or *complex*?

5. Michelle wants to be a nurse and her sister wants to be a doctor.
   _____

WEEK 21
ACTIVITY 2
TOTAL /5

Name: _____

Write the superlative and comparative forms of this adjective.

1. serious   _____   _____

Correct these sentences.

2. these is yore books on the tabel and them on the shelv is mine
   _____

3. chloe werks at pizza palace on monday and wednesday nites and on saturdays
   _____

Is the following text a complete sentence, or a fragment?

4. My favourite science fiction book   _____

5. That's really cool!   _____

WEEK 21
ACTIVITY 3
TOTAL /5

Name: _____

Correct these sentences.

1. miss vogel readed the pome the lady of shalott by alfred lord tennyson to are class
   _____

2. it are a sad tail about a young womin who escapes her prisin on a iland
   _____

Is the *predicate* in each sentence simple or compound?

3. We put the apples we picked into basket.   _____

4. One basket tipped over and the apples rolled out onto the ground.   _____

Choose the best word to complete this sentence.

5. The librarian asked us to speak ____.   more quietly / more quieter / most quiet

WEEK 21
ACTIVITY 4
TOTAL /5

Name: _____

Complete the analogies.

WEEK **21**

ACTIVITY **5**

TOTAL **/5**

1. Space is to rocket as _____ is to boat.

2. Mechanic is to motors as plumber is to _____

3. Fame is to famous as study is to _____

4. Brake is to stop as engine is to _____

5. Page is to book as _____ is to Canada.

Name: _____

Bonus Activity: Comparing Adjectives

WEEK **21**

Write the *comparative* and *superlative* forms for these adjectives.

1. quiet _____ _____   3. dreamy _____ _____

2. serious _____ _____   4. classy _____ _____

Write *antonyms* for these comparative and superlative adjective forms.

5. fastest _____   9. coarser _____

6. richer _____   10. smaller _____

7. thickest _____   11. narrower _____

8. best _____   12. tallest _____

MY CANADA

During the 1950s and 1960s, the makers of Canada Dry soft drinks marketed two new products: sugar-free beverages and soft drinks in cans – a first in the industry.

Name: _____

WEEK 22
ACTIVITY 1
TOTAL /5

Underline the *past participle* in each sentence.

1. By the time Harvey reached home, he had driven 300 kilometres.

2. He has worked in Toronto for three years now.

How many syllables does this word have?

3. mountaineer _____

Correct these sentences.

4. this here year the whether have bean colder in febraury than in january

   _____

5. people who likes winter sports like sking and skateing enjoy the cold whether

   _____

Name: _____

WEEK 22
ACTIVITY 2
TOTAL /5

Underline the double negative in this sentence. Then write the correct form to be used.

1. I haven't got no time to wait for you. _____

Underline the *subordinate clause* in each sentence.

2. If your tooth is still hurting, call the dentist.

3. He had already left when I returned from the store.

Correct these sentences.

4. watch out called jackie that their step are broken in too plases

   _____

5. thanks for werning me said anne i didnt sea enything rong

   _____

Name: _____

Underline the subordinating conjunction in each sentence.

1. Although it was carefully planned, the fundraiser was not a success.

2. You will need to study until you know all those multiplication facts.

Circle the words that have four syllables.

3. government   interfering   threatening   fertilizer

Correct these sentences.

4. we was gonna attand the game but the whether fourcaster sayed it were frezing reign
   _____

5. my dad rifuses to drive in bad whether becuz he says him has no cantrol over the car
   _____

WEEK 22
ACTIVITY 3
TOTAL /5

Name: _____

Underline the *linking verb* in this sentence.

1. Some desert areas are cold.
   _____

Correct these sentences.

2. entering the store fred walked don the center isle too the puzzles shelf
   _____

3. the car showne on the broshure was an knew modle chevrolay
   _____

Use context clues to explain the meaning of the underlined words.

4. The <u>mangy</u>, old dog just showed up on our doorstep.
   _____

5. The <u>distraught</u> mother was calling for help to find her child.
   _____

WEEK 22
ACTIVITY 4
TOTAL /5

Rewrite this short paragraph, correcting all the punctuation errors.

The frankfurter named for the city of frankfurt germany is easily the most popular sausage in the world frankfurters more commonly known as hot dogs are sold almost everywhere in north america they are a favourite food at sporting events amusement parks and fairs what family barbeque would be complete without hot dogs you might enjoy one with ketchup relish or mustard or even eat it plain do you think other people of the world enjoy hot dogs as much as canadians do

WEEK 22

ACTIVITY 5

TOTAL /5

Bonus Activity: What's Next?

Finish the story below by writing a short conclusion. Illustrate the story.

We had an incredible thunderstorm last night. The rain sounded like beating drums on our roof. The thunder was so loud all of our windows rattled. Lightning lit up the yard. During the storm, we heard a huge crash. I looked outside and saw...

My Conclusion

My Illustration

WEEK 22

MY CANADA — Missed some of the action? Not to worry. Instant replay was invented by the CBC in 1955. The technique was first used (where else?) on a broadcast of *Hockey Night in Canada*.

Name: _____

Correct these sentences.

1. gen stevens were a commandar dering world war l in england

   _____

2. because marianne and tina injoy dance they goes to meny performences

   _____

Underline the *correlative conjunctions* in this sentence.

3. You may chose either to go to the movies or have a sleepover for your birthday.

Circle the *antecedent* of the underlined pronoun.

4. The salmon swims upstream to lay its eggs.

5. Jack cleaned his room and closet too.

WEEK 23 — ACTIVITY 1 — TOTAL /5

Name: _____

Correct these sentences.

1. in an unanimous vote lizzy were declaired the knew class presadent

   _____

2. my naybors vicki and ross is moving to cold lake alberta in october

   _____

Underline the *complete subject* in each sentence.

3. A perfect, shiny, red apple grew near the top of the tree.

4. Todd climbed the ladder so he could pick it.

Add a *prefix* to make a new word.

5. violent   _____

WEEK 23 — ACTIVITY 2 — TOTAL /5

Name: _____

WEEK 23 — ACTIVITY 3 — TOTAL /5

Correct these sentences.

1. look out called pete the wagin of would are tipping over

   _____

2. joe didnt feel vary good after he eated fore hotdogs and drunk too drinks

   _____

Underline the *subordinate clause* in this sentence.

3. Hugh said he was walking to school alone, so we left without him.

Underline the *predicate adjectives* in each sentence.

4. The ceremony was simple and tasteful.

5. The soft snow looked fluffy and light.

Name: _____

WEEK 23 — ACTIVITY 4 — TOTAL /5

Underline the helping, or *auxiliary*, verb in this sentence.

1. I don't know where mom and dad have gone.

Is the tense of the underlined verb is *present, past,* or *future*?

2. I <u>will hike</u> to the top of the mountain.

3. My dad <u>hiked</u> there when he was my age.

Correct these sentences.

4. on may 21 2013 my ant bonnie graderated from dalhousie university

   _____

5. we had an selebrashun and evryone wish her all the best in her knew carer

   _____

Name: _____

Is each sentence is *declarative, interrogative, imperative,* or *exclamatory*?

WEEK 23
ACTIVITY 5
TOTAL /5

1. Have a cold glass of water to help you cool off. _____

2. The chocolate cupcakes are totally delicious! _____

3. Does Emma know anyone at her new school? _____

4. Grandma cooks a turkey dinner for us on Thanksgiving Sunday.
   _____

5. Call me if you need help with your math homework. _____

Name: _____

Bonus Activity: Gender Nouns Crossword

WEEK 23

Gender nouns tell us whether the noun refers to a masculine or feminine person.

Across
1. not the king but the ___
2. not an actress but an ___
3. not a woman but a ___
4. not the heiress but the ___
5. not your nephew but your ___
6. not your brother but your ___
7. not your aunt but your ___

Down
1. not a waiter but a ___
2. not a god but a ___
4. not a granddaughter but a ___
5. not the groom but the ___

MY CANADA The house at 128 Day Avenue in Toronto may hold the record as Canada's tiniest house. It is 2.2 metres wide and 14.3 meters long.

Name: _____

Circle the best word to complete this sentence.

1. These pencils belong to me. They are _____ . **me / mines / my / mine.**

Correct these sentences.

2. hour class is creting a play based on o henrys the ransom of red chief
   _____

3. it are a humerous story about a bad behaved boy and too simple fellows
   _____

Add a prefix to these words to make new words.

4. regular _____

5. known _____

WEEK 24
ACTIVITY 1
TOTAL /5

Name: _____

Underline the *simple subject*. Tell whether it is simple or compound.

1. The crafty magician pulled a rabbit and a dove out of his hat. _____

2. The boys and girls clapped and cheered at this trick. _____

Correct these sentences.

3. hour volunteers well werk all day saturday to cleen up the playground at hyde park
   _____

4. we well be cuting the grass pickin up trassh fixin the swings and painting the benchs
   _____

Is this sentence *declarative, interrogative, imperative,* or *exclamatory*?

5. It is a miracle that everyone survived that car crash! _____

WEEK 24
ACTIVITY 2
TOTAL /5

Is the following a fragment, or a complete sentence?

1. faster than a horse can run _____

Correct these sentences.

2. were gonna upgrade ours computer so its more faster
   _____

3. we is goin shoping on friday at computer world on brock street
   _____

Circle the *direct object* in each sentence.

4. Grandma put the flowers in a beautiful vase.

5. She picked asters and daisies from her own garden.

WEEK 24 — ACTIVITY 3 — TOTAL /5

Correct these sentences.

1. yes annie said mom i maked chockalate cake for tonites desert
   _____

2. did you puts chockalate ore vanella icing on it i asked
   _____

Underline the *verb* in each sentence.

3. The weather becomes cooler in September and October.

4. After that we can expect the snow to start falling.

Write the plural form of these nouns.

5. address _____ goalie _____

WEEK 24 — ACTIVITY 4 — TOTAL /5

Name: _____

Explain the meaning of these metaphors in your own words.

1. We need to find a way to <u>break the ice</u> with the new students in our class.
   _____

2. This homework is hard so I will need to <u>put my nose to the grindstone</u>.
   _____

3. What a close race! Danny won <u>by a hair</u>!
   _____

4. My grandpa enjoys a good joke as we know from his <u>belly laugh</u>.
   _____

5. The boss gave his workers <u>a tongue-lashing</u> for being so careless on the job.
   _____

WEEK 24
ACTIVITY 5
TOTAL /5

Name: _____

Bonus Activity: Natural Resources

Pollution is a problem that affects all people on the Earth. **Match the definition with the correct word. Put a star beside the ones that add to pollution.**

____ 1. A tanker runs aground and leaks oil

____ 2. Food for gardens from leaves and grass clippings.

____ 3. Poisonous materials like paint thinner.

____ 4. Energy generated from inside the Earth.

____ 5. Smoke and exhaust that mix with water vapour.

____ 6. Exhaust from cars and pollution from factories that create a layer in the atmosphere. Heat rays from the sun cannot go back into the atmosphere.

a) greenhouse effect
b) oil spill
c) geothermal energy
d) hazardous waste
e) compost
f) acid rain

WEEK 24
BONUS ACTIVITY

MY CANADA The *Newfoundland dog* is a made-in-Canada breed. The species was first named in the 17th century. The Newfoundland was originally used as a ship dog to carry lines to shore or for water rescues.

Name: _____

Correct these sentences.

1. Wen a lickwid are heated it releses vapors explaned mr clark
   _____

2. meny lickwids he continud tern to a soled wen that is cooled
   _____

Underline the *complete subject* and circle the *simple subject*.

3. Delicious, cinnamon smells filled the air.

4. Our talented sister cooks many treats for us.

Underline the *prepositions* in this sentence.

5. We heard the noise of the branches falling on the roof of our house.

WEEK 25
ACTIVITY 1
TOTAL /5

Name: _____

Correct these sentences.

1. dering this hear month i needs to go to my mothers ofice after sckool
   _____

2. my dad are tyed up with buziness meatings and arent home vary erly at nite
   _____

Write the base (or *root*) word for these words.

3. decision _____   gangster _____

How many syllables in each word?

4. Maniwaki _____

5. Wabakimi _____

WEEK 25
ACTIVITY 2
TOTAL /5

Name: _____

Underline the *present participle* in each sentence.

1. We are planning a big family dinner for Thanksgiving.

2. Relatives are coming from far away for the event.

Correct these sentences.

3. i just seen the cuttest little puppys at sam's pet shop exclamed fiona
   _____

4. i think i is gonna ask my parants if thay wood consitter leting me get one she addded
   _____

Rewrite this phrase using a *possessive noun*.

5. the sharp claws belonging to the cat _____

WEEK 25
ACTIVITY 3
TOTAL /5

Name: _____

Correct these sentences.

1. all the grad 7 lockers is on the ferst flore in the hall next to the jim
   _____

2. try to kep yore locker neet sew you is abel to find yore books quikly
   _____

Write the root word for:

3. musician _____

Underline the *independent clause* in each sentence.

4. When my friend Yan came to Canada, she couldn't speak any English.

5. She tried hard each day so she could learn more words.

WEEK 25
ACTIVITY 4
TOTAL /5

Name: _____

Combine the following sentences to make one good sentence.

WEEK 25
ACTIVITY 5
TOTAL /5

1. Ms Blair is our math teacher. She gives us lots of homework every night.
   _____

2. I looked for Jake at the movie. He wasn't there. He had stayed home instead.
   _____

3. Dawn and Audrey are spending the weekend in Montreal. They are visiting their cousins.
   _____

4. Island is the story of young teens on a ship. They are troubled kids who need help.
   _____

5. I am having a sleepover on Saturday night. We will have pizza. We will have chips too.
   _____

Name: _____

Bonus Activity: Saint-Pierre and Miguelon

Read the paragraph. Circle T if the sentence is true and F if it is false.

WEEK 25

There is a little piece of Europe right next to Canada. There are several small islands off the coast of Newfoundland where people sing "La Marseillaise" instead of "O Canada", speak a kind of French that is not spoken in Quebec and use Euros for their money. This unique territory is called Saint-Pierre and Miguelon, has belonged to France since 1763. It includes some smaller islands as well and has about 6500 residents. There are two airports located on the island, so you can fly there from Newfoundland, Nova Scotia, New Brunswick and Montreal. There is regular ferry service from Fortune, Newfoundland. Wouldn't this be an unusual place to visit?

1. T F Saint-Pierre and Miguelon belong to France.
2. T F Canadian dollars are used by the residents.
3. T F Only 3500 people live on the islands.

MY CANADA

On September 29, 1962, Canada became the third nation in space (after the USA and Russia). We launched the research satellite *Alouette*. It was designed to last for one year but performed without any trouble for the next 10 years.

Name: _____

WEEK 26 ACTIVITY 1

Explain these idioms.

1. Thank you for helping. You're <u>an angel in disguise</u>. _____

2. That explanation is as <u>clear as a bell</u>. _____

Correct these sentences.

3. maggie and pete is lerning how to skatebord at the hawkins youth center
   _____

4. a teem of skatebordes are teaching them how to be save and has fun two
   _____

Circle the *antecedent* of the underlined pronoun.

5. Polly and Hector went to the museum with <u>their</u> class.

TOTAL /5

Name: _____

WEEK 26 ACTIVITY 2

Add a prefix and a suffix to make two new words for each word.

1. allow   prefix _____   suffix _____

2. like   prefix _____   suffix _____

Circle the *direct object* and underline the *indirect object* in this sentence.

3. Janice wrote a human interest story for the local newspaper.

Correct these sentences.

4. wow look at them their awesum baskitball shews exclaimed franco
   _____

5. i dont gots enuf muney for those shews i replyed
   _____

TOTAL /5

Name: _____

Underline the *auxiliary*, or helping, verbs in these sentences.

1. If you have looked everywhere for your jacket, then it must be lost.

2. You will have some dessert when you have eaten you vegetables.

Correct these sentences.

3. that there book are a good story about an advenchure on a ship
   _____

4. i likes advenchure and misstery storys best espeshally if them are true
   _____

Is the tense of the verb in this sentence *past*, *present*, or *future*?

5. The princess dreamed of a Prince Charming.

WEEK 26
ACTIVITY 3
TOTAL /5

Name: _____

Correct these sentences.

1. if your hungry after school have some yogert selery or popcorn to ate
   _____

2. eric wilson author of meny canadian novels like to viset classrooms
   _____

Circle the *correlative conjunctions* in these sentences.

3. She broke her arm when she fell off her bicycle.

4. Because her arm needed to heal, she had a cast on it.

Underline the present tense verbs in this sentence.

5. When the game ends, everyone claps and cheers.

WEEK 26
ACTIVITY 4
TOTAL /5

Name: _____

Write the *simple subject* and the *simple predicate* for each sente

WEEK 26 — **ACTIVITY 5** — **TOTAL /5**

1. The judge awarded the first prize to my friend Amy.
   simple subject: _____ simple predicate: _____

2. The ancient castle looked out over the bay.
   simple subject: _____ simple predicate: _____

3. Conservation of energy receives much attention from scientists.
   simple subject: _____ simple predicate: _____

4. Our family is buying our Christmas gifts early this year.
   simple subject: _____ simple predicate: _____

5. The cold, wet rain fell for two days.
   simple subject: _____ simple predicate: _____

Name: _____

Bonus Activity: I Will Follow You ...

WEEK 26

Some verbs are followed by a preposition to make them correct. **Write the preposition that goes with each of the verbs.** The first one has been done.

1. belong <u>to</u>
2. hint _____
3. scoff _____
4. refer _____
5. listen _____
6. lead _____
7. stare _____
8. side _____
9. sympathize _____
10. consist _____
11. depend _____
12. glance _____
13. agree _____
14. laugh _____

MY CANADA

The ice storm that started on January 5, 1998, has been called *"the storm of the century"*. Six days of freezing rain led to month-long power outages in some areas. Estimated losses in insurance costs are a total of $2 billion.

WEEK 27 — ACTIVITY 1

Correct these sentences.

1. opin yore mouth and say ah said the dentest

_____

2. you has too cavitys that needs to be felled as soon as possable

_____

Underline the *subordinate clause* in each sentence.

3. After you set the table, call your brother to come in.

4. We will eat as soon as your mother gets home from work.

Is this sentence *declarative, interrogative, imperative,* or *exclamatory*?

5. Change your clothes and come with me.

TOTAL /5

WEEK 27 — ACTIVITY 2

Underline the *predicate adjectives* in each sentence.

1. In autumn, leaves turn red, yellow, orange and brown.

2. The bread smelled garlicky and delicious.

Number these words in alphabetical order

3. ___ loud   ___ lots   ___ lottery   ___ lovely   ___ lower   ___ load

Correct these sentences.

4. we needs to find sum informashun about canadas lumbering indestry

_____

5. doenst you no the bested places to look for fax about this here topic

_____

TOTAL /5

Name: _____

Use context clues to explain the meaning of the underlined words.

1. Seth was gratified when his teacher praised his report.
   _____

2. That little boy is becoming a nuisance with his water pistol.
   _____

Correct these sentences.

3. we has a wunderful suprise today ms southern telled her kindergarden class
   _____

4. sparky the fire safety dog are comin to viset us and tell us how to bee safe
   _____

Circle the *direct object* and underline the *indirect object* in this sentence.

5. Because we won, our coach bought everyone pizza and soft drinks.

WEEK 27
ACTIVITY 3
TOTAL /5

Name: _____

Explain the meaning of this idiom.

1. If you face trouble, try to keep a stiff upper lip.

Correct these sentences.

2. nobodies is sure what happened to toms bike witch he leaved outside last nite
   _____

3. after there daylong nape the cats runned up and down the stares all nite
   _____

Tell if the sentence is *simple, compound,* or *complex.*

4. Because she had an earache, Susie went to the doctor. _____

5. Finish writing your test and hand in your papers. _____

WEEK 27
ACTIVITY 4
TOTAL /5

Name: _____

Adverbs can show time. **Write each adverb from the Word Box under the correct heading.**

| next | today | tomorrow | after | now | recently |
| later | yesterday | presently | earlier | currently | before |

Present	Past	Future

WEEK **27**

ACTIVITY **5**

TOTAL **/5**

Name: _____

Bonus Activity: Give Me a "C"

Below are the names of places in Canada that start with the letter C. **Find and circle the following words in the puzzle.**

Cabonga	Cambridge
Camrose	Chapleau
Chatham	Churchill
Calgary	Cornwall
Canso	Champlain
Chilliwack	Clarenville

c	h	i	l	l	i	w	a	c	k	s	c
a	c	l	l	a	w	n	r	o	c	c	h
m	a	i	u	a	e	l	p	a	h	c	a
b	l	n	d	e	i	a	e	a	u	c	m
r	g	l	h	o	g	n	t	c	r	a	p
i	a	i	c	n	o	h	a	a	c	m	l
d	r	u	o	n	a	n	e	e	h	r	a
g	y	e	o	n	a	n	p	l	h	r	a
e	a	d	a	o	w	t	u	a	l	s	n
c	l	a	r	e	n	v	i	l	l	e	s

WEEK **27**

MY CANADA

In 1908, *P.E.I. banned the use of cars* on its roads. Many islanders thought the automobile was too noisy and scared the horses. The ban was finally lifted in 1918.

Name: _____

Circle the best word or words to complete these sentences.

WEEK 28
ACTIVITY 1

1. Jay said he sings the ___ of anyone he knows.   **most bad / worst / worser**

2. We waited ___ for him to arrive.   **patientlier / more patiently / patiently**

Correct these sentences.

3. the bronson family builded a knew house on the cornar of archer street and bay street

_____

4. hey Id like to joine in that there game youse is playing said mark

_____

TOTAL /5

How many syllables in each word?

5. ptarmigan _____   whippoorwill _____

Name: _____

Is the underlined text a complete sentence, or a fragment?

WEEK 28
ACTIVITY 2

1. They have moved to a new apartment. <u>It is very small</u>. _____

Correct these sentences.

2. the littl buoy screemed i went my mommy rite now

_____

3. duz enyone has a idea for hour sceince project asked terri

_____

TOTAL /5

Underline the *predicate adjectives*.

4. Henry's sports car is small but powerful.

5. Your stories are funny, unusual and entertaining.

Name: _____

Underline the *prepositional phrase* and circle the *direct object* of the preposition.

WEEK **28**

1. The sock with the hole belongs to my brother.

2. We sat at a picnic table in the peaceful park.

ACTIVITY **3**

Underline the *synonyms* in the following sentence.

3. The scenes in that movie were gruesome but the sound effects were even more horrible.

TOTAL **/5**

Correct these sentences.

4. the bailey kids wants a puppy there parants aint so shure about the idea
_____

5. chloe our next dore naybor are playing soceer in the greenville girls league
_____

Name: _____

Write the plural for these nouns.

WEEK **28**

1. boss _____   wax _____

Correct these sentences.

ACTIVITY **4**

2. peggy our cousen from moose jaw lost wait becuz she startid runnin
_____

TOTAL **/5**

3. historiens beleive that them there vikings was the ferst visiters to canada
_____

Tell the gender of these nouns. Write M for Masculine and F for Female.

4. gander _____

5. doe _____

Name: _____

A verb is in *active voice* when the subject performs the action. A verb is in *passive voice* when the subject receives the action. Change these sentences from passive to active voice.

1. Sunglasses were invented many years ago by the Inuit.
   _____

2. A pair made from walrus ivory was found by hunters in Baffin, Quebec.
   _____

3. A tiny slit was cut in the bone or antlers by carvers to make the sunglasses.
   _____

4. These sunglasses were used by the Inuit to protect against snow blindness.
   _____

5. The sunglasses can be seen by visitors to the Canadian Museum of Civilization.
   _____

WEEK 28
ACTIVITY 5
TOTAL /5

Name: _____

Bonus Activity: I'm So Confused ?????

Decide which word to use in each sentence. Write your answer on the line.

1. I should have heeded his _____ and stayed out of trouble. **advise / advice**

2. They will _____ the seeds when the weather warms up. **sew / sow**

3. The 12 children will share the snacks _____ them. **among / between**

4. We all laughed at the _____ of him in the funny costume. **site / sight**

5. Please _____ your hand before you speak. **raise / rise**

6. He didn't seem to realize how that would _____ him. **affect / effect**

7. They did not intend to _____ the original plan. **altar / alter**

WEEK 28

MY CANADA The first zoo in North America was opened in Halifax in 1847. Known as Down's Zoological Gardens, it was home to a large collection of birds, animals and plants. It was later sold and became the Central Park Zoo in New York.

Name: _____

WEEK 29

ACTIVITY 1

TOTAL /5

Correct these sentences.

1. visiters two quebec city like to fotograph the meny old hisstorick buildings
   _____

2. we needs to finnish hour homewerk take a shour and washes hour hare
   _____

Add a suffix to change these words to nouns.

3. king   _____

4. amuse   _____

Underline the *prepositional phrase* in this sentence.

5. The rabbit in the cage was twitching its nose.

Name: _____

WEEK 29

ACTIVITY 2

TOTAL /5

Correct these sentences.

1. canada has the largist coliny of atlantic puffins in north america
   _____

2. it are finded in newfoundland's witless bay ecological reserve
   _____

Use context clues to explain the meaning of the underlined words.

3. We will soon have to <u>wean</u> the puppies from their mother.
   _____

4. They will use a bulldozer to <u>excavate</u> a big hole.
   _____

***Synonyms* or *antonyms*?**

5. runaway, fugitive   _____

Name: _____

Correct these sentences.

1. These hear cookys looks delishus but is they peanut free asked ali

   _____

2. mollys ferst viset to winnipeg were on july 1 2006 wen she were six years olde

   _____

Underline the *linking verb* in each sentence.

3. The music coming from his bedroom was too loud.

4. I got up early so the day seemed longer than usual.

Is the underlined text a complete sentence, or fragment?

5. She is learning to skate. <u>But not very well right now</u>. _____

WEEK 29
ACTIVITY 3
TOTAL /5

Name: _____

Underline the *object of the preposition* in each sentence.

1. People in the news are often embarrassed by the reports of the press.

2. The drugstore in our town is open for business for six days of the week.

Correct these sentences.

3. we is going to landon bay to join a conservation program called local wildlife

   _____

4. they will teach all about how to proteck anamals nativ plants and berds

   _____

Underline the *interjection* in this sentence.

5. Oh no! This is terrible!

WEEK 29
ACTIVITY 4
TOTAL /5

Name: _____

Put brackets ( ) around the *prepositional phrase* and underline the *subordinate clauses*.

WEEK **29**

ACTIVITY **5**

TOTAL **/5**

1. <u>As the last of the guests left,</u> she gave a sigh (of relief).

2. <u>If you do not follow the rules,</u> you may be (in trouble).

3. Good friends are helpers (in time) of trouble.

4. (In the last few minutes), our team won the game.

5. The crowd cheered <u>as the monkey performed his tricks.</u>

Name: _____

Bonus Activity: Where Do I Look?

WEEK **29**

There are many sources of information we can use. **Pick a reference source from this list to match the phrases to tell where you would look for information.**

| encyclopedia | cookbook | atlas | thesaurus | dictionary | almanac |

1. the pronunciation of the word "courier" _____

2. a recipe for making homemade bread _____

3. another word for "trouble" _____

4. the location of the Ungava Peninsula _____

5. an antonym for "interesting" _____

MY CANADA *The Canadian Canoe Museum* in Peterborough, Ontario, is home to the world's largest collection of canoes and kayaks. Founded in 1997, it has more than 600 boats in its collection.

Name: _____

Circle the *auxiliary*, or helping, verbs in this sentence.

1. Our town is building a new library and the community is donating books for it.

Correct these sentences.

2. even tho i heared that there story befour i still listend for the suprise ending
   _____

3. wood you like to reed a story by the same auther asked the libarian
   _____

Circle the direct object and underline the indirect object in these sentences.

4. Jeff gave me a free ticket to his hockey game tonight.

5. The book won her instant fame.

WEEK 30
ACTIVITY 1
TOTAL /5

Name: _____

Is the underlined verb *transitive* or *intransitive*?

1. The little boy cried because he scraped his knee. _____

Correct these sentences.

2. on a beutiful autome day i like to strole threw the woods and colleckt leafs
   _____

3. somtimes i puts them in books to press them so i cans make a dispaly
   _____

Circle the best word to complete each sentence.

4. These bracelets belong to Susan. They are _____.   **her / theirs / hers / their**

5. That jacket belongs to Wendy. It is _____.   **her / ours / hers / our**

WEEK 30
ACTIVITY 2
TOTAL /5

Name: _____

Correct these sentences.

1. max and ruby are a poplar tv show for young childrun it are on every day

   _____

2. i perfer to watch natchure shows like wild kingdom or strange and unusual anamals

   _____

Underline the *prepositional phrase* in this sentence.

3. The old friends sat under the shady tree and visited.

Underline the *predicate adjectives* in these sentences.

4. Our new principal seems strict but fair.

5. She is popular with all the students.

WEEK 30
ACTIVITY 3
TOTAL /5

Name: _____

Correct these sentences.

1. sun blocke are impotent to remembr to brang to the beech

   _____

2. bring sum sanwitches froot pickels and drinks and well have a picknick

   _____

Write the base, or *root*, word for this word.

3. unhappiness _____

***Declarative, interrogative, imperative, or exclamatory*?**

4. An avalanche struck the village last night. _____

5. Is the rescue team still at the site? _____

WEEK 30
ACTIVITY 4
TOTAL /5

Name: _____

Decide if the underlined word is an *adjective* or a *pronoun*. Write Pronoun or Adjective on the line following each sentence.

1. <u>Some</u> slang is acceptable in ordinary speech. _____

2. <u>Everyone</u> attended the rally yesterday. _____

3. <u>This</u> will soon be past history. _____

4. <u>Somebody</u> has already been assigned to do that job. _____

5. <u>Most</u> people will obey that sign. _____

WEEK 30

ACTIVITY 5

TOTAL /5

Name: _____

Bonus Activity: Money! Money

Place the following words in each of the categories below.

nickel peso pay wallet bank account franc loonie cash register invest dime collect quarter safe save toonie ruble bank earn shilling spend lira yen cheque vault

Units of money	Places to keep $$$
Foreign Money	What We Do with $$$

WEEK 30

MY CANADA

The Dionne Quintuplets were born in Corbeil, Ontario on May 28, 1934. They were the first quintuplets in the world to survive for more that a few days. They became a big tourist attraction in Canada at that time.

Name: _____

Circle the *conjunction* in each sentence.

1. We will understand the lives of early people if we study their history.

2. Toronto, which is a large city, is a commercial, cultural, and communications centre.

Correct these sentences.

3. mavis colleckts old stamps she havs meny from asian countrys
   _____

4. sumtimes she finds old stamps at yard sails or at awkshuns
   _____

Is the underlined verb *transitive* or *intransitive*?

5. The tower collapsed to the ground.

WEEK 31 — ACTIVITY 1 — TOTAL /5

Name: _____

Underline the *present participle* in each sentence.

1. The wind created some cooling breezes for the runners.
2. We knew he was scared from his shaking knees.

Correct these sentences.

3. josie you dont loose yore tickit to the consert ore you wont be abel to go
   _____

4. tomorow is pitch in day said mr grove so come dressed in olde close
   _____

Write the plural form for each noun.

5. switch _____   mosquito _____

WEEK 31 — ACTIVITY 2 — TOTAL /5

Name: _____

Underline the *independent clauses* in these sentences.

1. Because she has allergies, Allison can't have pets.

2. Our team is going to the tournament if we win the next game.

Circle the *subject* of this sentence.

3. Pause the movie so I can get some snacks.   **I / they / we / you**

Correct these sentences.

4. nova scotia on canadas atlantic coast have the hire tieds in the world

   _____

5. peggys cove are visited bye thousands of turists each year

   _____

WEEK **31**
ACTIVITY **3**
TOTAL **/5**

Name: _____

Underline the *predicate adjectives* in this sentence.

1. The tomatoes in my garden are round, juicy and delicious.

Correct these sentences.

2. the beaver hour locale newspaper runned a article on soler power

   _____

3. sum people is installing soler panals on theyre proparty to preduce electricity

   _____

Circle the *auxiliary*, or helping, verb in each sentence.

4. All the monarch butterflies have flown south.

5. In the spring, they will return.

WEEK **31**
ACTIVITY **4**
TOTAL **/5**

Name: _____

Change these sentences from passive to active voice.

1. The ice was cleaned by the zamboni.
   _____

2. The rookie player was honoured by the team.
   _____

3. Much enjoyment has been given by their performance.
   _____

4. We were told the news of the fire by our neighbours.
   _____

5. Paul was presented with the Volunteer of the Year Award by the committee.
   _____

WEEK **31**

ACTIVITY **5**

TOTAL /5

Name: _____

Bonus Activity: Order! Order!

Number these sentences in the correct order to form a paragraph.

____ On October 17, 1878, Sir John A. Macdonald became Prime Minister for the second time.

____ In 1830, Macdonald began studying law with a prominent Kingston lawyer.

____ John A. Macdonald was born on January 11, 1815, in Glasgow, Scotland.

____ In 1929, at the age of fourteen, he finished his formal schooling.

____ In 1820, his family moved to Canada when he was five years old and settled in Kingston, Upper Canada.

____ In 1836, he was admitted to the bar of Upper Canada and began to practice law.

____ In 1867, Macdonald became the first prime Minister of the Dominion of Canada.

WEEK **31**

MY CANADA — On January 22, 1992, Dr. Roberta Bondar, a native of Sault Ste. Marie, Ontario, became the first Canadian woman in space and the second Canadian to leave the planet.

Name: _____

Correct these sentences.

1. meny first nations canadians lived a harsh live in erly times

   _____

2. thay servied by huntin and fishin and growin there own food

   _____

Circle the best word to complete this sentence.

3. March is often ___ than April. **most windy / windier / windiest / more windy**

Subject pronoun or *object pronoun*?

4. <u>Everyone</u> wants to be his friend.   _____

5. We asked <u>them</u> to come over for dinner.   _____

WEEK 32
ACTIVITY 1
TOTAL /5

Name: _____

Is this sentence *simple, compound,* or *complex*?

1. Leslie and Luke are organizing the fundraiser.   _____

Correct these sentences.

2. ms redford i gots to leaf class erly and go to meat my mom i said

   _____

3. thats fine ms redford replyed watch the clock and leaf when you needs too go

   _____

Underline the *conjunctions* in these sentences. Are they coordinating or subordinating?

4. Either Dodi or Penny will wash the dishes tonight.   _____

5. Although she is tired, my sister will help me with my homework.

   _____

WEEK 32
ACTIVITY 2
TOTAL /5

Name: _____

Circle the word that best fits into each sentence.

1. Lassie was a dog _____ starred in movies.   **who / that**

2. Your jacket is different _____ your sister's.   **from / than**

Correct these sentences.

3. sense they is grounded wally and jim wont do nothing to upset there parants

_____

4. a wrinkle in time is a favorit story of mine to reed

_____

Circle the compound subject and underline the compound predicate.

5. The boys and girls will sing and dance at the talent show.

WEEK 32
ACTIVITY 3
TOTAL /5

Name: _____

Circle the *direct object* and underline the *indirect object* in this sentence.

1. Her parents gave Janet a kitten for her birthday.

Correct these sentences.

2. wen mrs cook were sick we had helped with the cleening

_____

3. her appreshiated the kinerness of her naybors

_____

Underline the *subordinate clause* in each sentence.

4. The children dreamed of riding downhill while the snow fell outside.

5. After you finish your work, you may have a treat.

WEEK 32
ACTIVITY 4
TOTAL /5

Name: _____

Combine these sentences into one good sentence.

1. Finish writing your test. Check for errors. Hand it in.
   _____

2. Our house was damaged. It was the windstorm. A tree fell on our deck.
   _____

3. Sally made cookies yesterday. They were delicious. We ate them all.
   _____

4. Joe is a stamp collector. He trades with his friends. He buys some stamps at sales.
   _____

5. We will start soon. You need to be ready. You need a sharp pencil and a ruler.
   _____

WEEK 32
ACTIVITY 5
TOTAL /5

Name: _____

Bonus Activity: A Not-So-Secret Message!

Discover the message by using the code below.

!	@	#	$	%	^	&	*	(	)	=	_	+	:	;	"	'	<	,	>	.	?	/	[	\	]
a	b	c	d	e	f	g	h	i	j	k	l	m	n	o	p	q	r	s	t	u	v	w	x	y	z

" < ; . $ > ;   = (? %   (:   !   & < % ! >   # : . : > < \ .

Using the code above, write your own short message. Have a friend decrypt it.

WEEK 32

MY CANADA The last fatal duel in Canada occurred on May 22, 1838 in Verdun, Quebec. Major Henry Warde was fatally shot by lawyer Robert Sweeney. And what was Warde's offence? He wrote a love letter to Mrs. Sweeney.

ANSWER KEY

WEEK 1: ACTIVITY 1

1. Donna said, "My favourite TV Saturday show is <u>Dance Club</u>."
2. "I agree," replied Erica. "But I like <u>Austin and Ally</u> too."
3. Dan's and Marty's jackets
4. Please <u>stop</u> at the store and buy some fruit.
5. Our school soccer team <u>has</u> won all their games this season.

WEEK 1: ACTIVITY 2

1. She <u>doesn't</u> like that song on the radio.
2. Gerry and Tom asked Jim to bring his new glove to their baseball practice.
3. My parents are leaving tomorrow for their vacation to New Brunswick.
4. Jack's mother made his favourite chocolate <u>cake</u>.
5. My little cousin asks a lot of silly <u>questions</u>.

WEEK 1: ACTIVITY 3

1. Hwy.   2. RCMP
3. Let's have a movie party with popcorn, drinks, ice cream, and candy.
4. We could watch <u>Terror at the Top</u> and scare the girls.
5. We looked into the <u>stream</u> and saw tiny minnows.

WEEK 1: ACTIVITY 4

1. (Those boys) <u>practise every day for the cross-country race</u>.
2. (Determination and daily practice) <u>will help them to win</u>.
3. In 1535, Jacques Cartier sailed up the St. Lawrence River on his way to Quebec City.
4. His guides pointed out the way to "kanata" or "village" and he gave the land this name.
5. Jenna <u>has been</u> reading the book <u>Number the Stars</u>.

WEEK 1: ACTIVITY 5

1. Go away.
2. Don't make my success seem like nothing.
3. The centre of her life; most important part
4. It's easy.
5. Very early.

BONUS ACTIVITY: CAKE RECIPE PUZZLE

6, 1, 11, 2, 3, 8, 4, 9, 10, 5, 7, 12

WEEK 2: ACTIVITY 1

1. Jill received an A+ on her project called "Famous Canadian Authors".
2. I did my project on the Canadian invention the Canadarm.
3. axes   4. shelves
5. (My cousins, Ella and Emma,) <u>take tennis lessons every Saturday</u>.

WEEK 2: ACTIVITY 2

1. The woods looked <u>dark</u> and <u>dangerous</u>.
2. prefix : un   suffix : able
3. prefix :re   suffix : ed
4. So many beavers was killed during the fur trade that they were almost extinct by the 1800's.
5. When beaver hats went out of style, the beaver population recovered.

WEEK 2: ACTIVITY 3

1. Abby won a <u>medal</u> and some <u>money</u> at the art contest.
2. My sister Patricia, who goes to Queen's University, wants to be a doctor.
3. She wants to work with families in the Canadian Arctic if she can.
4. hero   5. child

WEEK 2: ACTIVITY 4

1. In the 1850's, people in Canada couldn't decide on where to put our capital city.
2. They asked Queen Victoria to decide and she picked Ottawa, Ontario .
3. singular possessive   4. plural possessive
5. When you get home, hang your jacket in the closet.

WEEK 2: ACTIVITY 5

1. simple   2. compound   3. complex
4. simple   5. complex

BONUS ACTIVITY: CONTEXT CLUES

1. Sings, chirps   2. Puzzled, confused   3. On time
4. Extremely important

WEEK 3: ACTIVITY 1

1. "It's an honour to meet you, Mrs. King," said Rachel.
2. "Thank you," said Mrs. King. "I am enjoying my visit

to your town."
3. <u>Deep inside the cave, the hunter</u> found the bear cub.
4. It was cold, hungry and lost.
5. Compound

Week 3: Activity 2

1. This beautiful bracelet was a gift <u>from my favourite aunt</u>.
2. She bought it while she was travelling in <u>British Columbia</u>.
3. "Will you be able to meet me at 3:00 p.m. at the movie theatre?" asked Harry.
4. I will buy our snacks. Do you want popcorn and a drink?
5. Before I start my homework, <u>I always get a snack to eat</u>.

Week 3: Activity 3

1. <u>I like the new student</u> even though I don't know him very well.
2. Whenever you have time, <u>I would like a copy of that recipe</u>.
3. Mr. Downes, the music teacher, called a band practice for after school tonight.
4. Be on time and bring your sheet music for our new number.
5. I made cherry chip <u>cupcakes</u> for my niece's (birthday).

Week 3: Activity 4

1. <u>If there is any ice cream in the freezer</u>, we will have it for a treat.
2. <u>If you go to bed too late</u>, you will be tired in the morning.
3. My cousin's name is Timothy James, but I call him T.J. for short.
4. He were born on August 21, 2000, in Edmonton, Alberta.
5. I went to the mall (and) bought a new pair of cleats (so) I would be ready for the game.

Week 3: Activity 5

1. Sandra muttered, "I'm never going to finish this report."
2. "Get all of the ingredients together first," Mom reminded me, "and then we will start to bake."
3. "We will still play hard," said Coach Drake, "even though some players are injured."
4. "Just keep trying," the voice inside my head whispered.
5. "You never know what you can do," said Dad, "until you are put to the test."

Bonus Activity: Simile or Metaphor?

1. Metaphor 2. Simile 3. Simile 4. Metaphor
5. Simile 6. Simile

Week 4: Activity 1

1. "What should we bring to the pot luck lunch on Friday?" asked Fred.
2. Scientists found a rare fossil of an insect in northern Manitoba.
3. Future 4. Past
5. she's

Week 4: Activity 2

1. The homemade fudge was <u>sweet</u> and gooey.
2. Imperative
3. (The jet-black horses) <u>pulled the golden carriage</u>.
4. The first version of O' Canada was written in French and performed in Quebec city in 1880.
5. O' Canada was named Canada's official national anthem in 1980.

Week 4: Activity 3

1. The <u>cat</u> jumped down and landed on its feet.
2. <u>Jimmy</u> took off <u>his</u> socks and shoes and waded into the water.
3. Jenny Jackson, our next door neighbour, is studying to be a nurse.
4. She hopes to get a job at Toronto Sick Kids Hospital.
5. desire

Week 4: Activity 4

1. Future 2. Past
3. The first chapter of <u>White Fang</u> is very exciting.
4. Have you ever thought of travelling to Canada's north?
5. On time; with just enough time

Week 4: Activity 5

1. Toronto is the biggest city in Canada but Ottawa is the capital city.
2. Mr. Quinn, our history teacher, is an expert on Confederation.
3. For breakfast, I love pancakes covered with delicious maple syrup.
4. Have you ever been across the Confederation Bridge that joins Nova Scotia and P.E.I.?
5. A cross-country trip would be exciting and educational.

Bonus Activity: Imagine This!

b	a	s	k	e	t	b	a	l	l			e			
t				e			a	i		s	u	p	e	r	m	a	n
v				l			c	g		q					c
				e			r	h	o	c	k	e	y		a
				p			o	t					i		n
				h			s	b				p			a
f	o	g	h	o	r	n	s	u				p			d
				n			e	l			e				a
				e				b		r					r
g	o	a	l	i	e	m	a	s	k						m

Week 5: Activity 1

1. The number of soccer fans is (growing) in Canada.
2. "Where do you want to go for our vacation this summer?" asked Dad.
3. "Let's visit some interesting places right around here," suggested Mom.
4. boys   5. Callie's poodle

Week 5: Activity 2

1. <u>You pick a movie to watch</u> while I make the popcorn.
2. Even though I don't like scary movies, <u>I will watch one with you.</u>
3. Those women did all the cooking for the Fairfield Annual Turkey Supper
4. For dessert, they made pies: blueberry, cherry, pumpkin, apple, lemon, and coconut cream.
5. Fragment

Week 5: Activity 3

1. I will call you <u>as soon as</u> I get home.
2. I'm going to the movies <u>but</u> I won't be late.
3. Big (cities) often have many tall buildings.
4. The first part of <u>Discovery North</u> was filmed in Hudson Bay.
5. Almost everybody on the film crew was from the Arctic or northern Ontario.

Week 5: Activity 4

1. Very fast
2. Aunt Sue, my dad's sister, is a nurse in Medicine Hat, Alberta.
3. She tries to visit our family each year at Christmas and Thanksgiving.
4. plural   5. singular

Week 5: Activity 5

1. "Come in," said Grandma. "I have made your favourite lunch."
2. "I have brought you a surprise from Mom," I said. "Can you guess what it is?"
3. "She is full of surprises," said Grandma. "But I have an idea what it is."
4. "Let's wait until after lunch to open it, okay?" I teased.
5. "Just how hungry are you?" Grandma teased me right back.

Bonus Activity: Concrete or Abstract?

Dad told Sam that today he was going to learn to ride his new bike. As Sam put his hands on the handlebars, Dad could see the fear on his face. Then Sam began to cry and big tears rolled down his cheeks. Dad held the bike as Sam pushed on the pedals. His balance was good and the bike started to move. Sam's concentration was paying off. Even his fear was going away. Suddenly, Dad let go without saying a word to Sam. Sam was riding all by himself. He didn't pick up much speed but he rode down the lane without any help. When Sam reached the end of the lane, he stopped and turned to his dad. With a big smile on his face, he yelled, "I did it!" Dad saw the pride on Sam's face. "Let's go tell your mother all about your accomplishment," he said.

Week 6: Activity 1

1. Henry spent the whole day at the beach with Uncle Brad from Vancouver.
2. They played Frisbee toss, made a huge sand castle, and swam for hours.
3. Sally writes short funny (stories) for children's <u>magazines</u>.
4. She donates her (fees) to the <u>Save the Children Fund</u>.
5. Crossbar Ranch's horses

Week 6: Activity 2

1. celebration: 4   magnificent: 4
2. future   3. past
4. Pete rode his bike faster than he has ever ridden before.
5. Until he falls off, he will ride faster and faster.

Week 6: Activity 3

1. He can't sing on key.
2. <u>Unless</u> you finish your chores, you won't be going to the movies.

3. We will wait on the corner until you get there.
4. Arctic wolves that live in Canada's North prey on caribou.
5. They travel in packs, chase their prey, surround them, and then attack.

Week 6: Activity 4

1. After you wash and dry the dishes, put them away on the shelves in the cupboard
2. Don't break any or you will be in big trouble with Grandma Rose.
3. (I) haven't learned this new dance because it is very complicated.
4. (I) need a good partner to help me with the steps.
5. you

Week 6: Activity 5

Did you know that all living things in our oceans are endangered by pollution? And who are the worst offenders? That's right, humans. Pollution can happen in many ways. One way is the dumping of waste materials, such as garbage and sewage, right into the ocean. An oil spill is another source of concern. Oil covers the gills of fish and causes them to smother. Birds get oil on their wings and are unable to fly. Do you know what happens when the birds try to clean oil off their wings? Often they get poisoned and die. Don't you agree that we should take steps to control pollution in our oceans?

Bonus Activity: A Big "Con"

1. congested   2. convince   3. consult
4. conservation   5. conscious   6. conclude

Week 7: Activity 1

1. Mom's Dutch apple pie won first prize at Farmersville Fair in July.
2. She developed this special recipe that is a family secret.
3. advertisement   4. direction
5. Our teacher told the class an exciting (story) about her trip to Australia.

Week 7: Activity 2

1. fragment   2. Complete sentence
3. We watched the comet streak across the night sky.
4. Susanna Moodie came to Upper Canada in 1832 from England.
5. She wrote a book called Roughing It in the Bush to tell of the hardships of pioneer life.

Week 7: Activity 3

1. Corporation: Corp.
2. Little Susie felt very proud when she got dressed all by herself.
3. There are many kinds of fish in Troy Lake, but perch is the most common.
4. Some (birds), like the ostrich, don't use their wings to fly.
5. (Ms. Murray), my teacher, parks her car by the fence.

Week 7: Activity 4

1. I've been learning to downhill ski, but I still fall down a lot.
2. My instructor, Jake Adams, is one of the best at Mt. Logan Lodge.
3. Skin is to human as feathers are to bird
4. Canada's Olympic gold medals
5. the old city's narrow streets

Week 7: Activity 5

1. Complex   2. Compound   3. Simple   4. Complex
5. Compound

Bonus Activity: Map It Out!

Check for setting/character details and speech balloons.

Week 8: Activity 1

1. Emily Howard Stowe was the first woman to practice medicine in Canada.
2. She faced many hardships but carried on in her effort to help others.
3. Dad reads the daily (newspaper) each night.
4. We bought cotton (candy) at the fair.
5. special: exceptional, extraordinary, unusual

Week 8: Activity 2

1. Read the instructions (and) follow them closely.
2. Dad tried (but) he was unable to fix my bike.
3. unfortunately: 5
4. My brother Ben wakes up the most early of all my family so he can run before school.
5. He hopes he can run in the Annual Jack Ross Marathon in September.

Week 8: Activity 3

1. navigation, navigator
2. obligation

3. Did you know that the first settlers in Newfoundland were Vikings?
4. "Yes I did," replied Allie. "I did a report called First Visitors to North America."
5. Our hike took us (into) the forest, (through) the trees, (across) a stream and (into) the field.

WEEK 8: ACTIVITY 4

1. The play, Stranger After Dark, which was a student production, was a great success.
2. Ellie Clarke played the heroine who rescued her best friend Danny from the stranger.
3. Some (people) avoid going to the dentist because they are afraid.
4. the van's snow tires   5. Grade 7's math books

WEEK 8: ACTIVITY 5

1. "Mom, I'm sorry I'm so late," Lily said sadly. "It won't happen again."
2. Paul shouted, "Last one in the pool is a rotten egg!"
3. "Ouch!" yelled Tim. "You hit my hand with that hammer."
4. "Linda and I are going shopping in Montreal this weekend," said Darcy.
5. "Have you ever read Storm Chaser ?" asked William.

BONUS ACTIVITY: WORDS! WORDS! WORDS!

Answers may vary. Suggestions are listed below.
Mrs. Crawford always wears beautiful jewellery. She owns many old (antique) pieces. For everyday wear, she often chooses more modern (contemporary) items. One day she noticed (observed) that some of her jewels had mysteriously (strangely) disappeared. She called the police and they agreed to check into it (investigate). After a short time, they had the answer (solution). A crow had carried them off to its nest in a nearby tree!

WEEK 9: ACTIVITY 1

1. Simple   2. Complex
3. Seventy- five million years ago, forests and warm seas covered most of Canada.
4. Huge dinosaurs roamed the earth looking for food and water.
5. Little (Mia) dresses up as a princess every chance she gets.

WEEK 9: ACTIVITY 2

1. She can't go out (because) she has to study for a history test.
2. (As long as) I have known her, school work comes first.
3. frogman: frogmen   reef: reefs
4. I wear sunglasses all year long because the sun hurts my eyes.
5. Instead of buying a house, they are going live in an apartment.

WEEK 9: ACTIVITY 3

1. Transitive
2. When the contestants give their speech, they will all sit on the stage.
3. "Only the first place winner will go on to the next level," said Ms. Franklin.
4. Oct.   5. CBS

WEEK 9: ACTIVITY 4

1. David, don't take any of those cookies or there won't be enough for lunch.
2. Janice was born in Cranbrook, British Columbia, but now she lives in Truro, Nova Scotia.
3. A kind of food with several ingredients, usually cooked in a deep dish.
4. The (sunshine) spread its warmth over my garden.
5. (Hallie) worked hard to win her award in swimming.

WEEK 9: ACTIVITY 5

1. If you want dessert, you must eat your dinner and drink your milk first.
2. Mr. Ducharme, Keira's grandfather, lives in Quebec but he visits her often.
3. Some dogs are great watchdogs but my dog Digger just sleeps all day.
4. Mom makes the best chocolate chip cookies using Grandma's recipe.
5. Little Tommy looked out the window and frowned because it was raining outside.

BONUS ACTIVITY: OH, LAND!

plateau/red	aluminum/green	iron/green	gulf/blue
nickel/green	prairie/red	strait/blue	diamond/green
gold/green	channel/blue	muskeg/red	uranium/green
rapids/blue	natural gas/green	oil/green	canyon/red

Week 10: Activity 1

1. Complete sentence   2. Fragment
3. Their phone rings much louder than most phones do.
4. "Eat your lunch," said Mrs. Bell, "and then you may go outside"
5. tornadoes   ferries

Week 10: Activity 2

1. Sometimes I (appear) not to be listening, but I am.
2. This food (smells) so good that it is making me hungry.
3. I dream of the <u>day</u> when I might travel on an <u>airplane</u> to <u>Scotland</u>.
4. Emily Murphy wrote popular books about early life in Canada.
5. Instead of using her own name, she used the pen name "Janey Canuck."

Week 10: Activity 3

1. fiercely
2. For this recipe, I'm going to use butter, milk, brown sugar, and two eggs.
3. Heat the oven to 350°, use a glass pan, and bake for at least 35 minutes.
4. Exclamatory   5. Imperative

Week 10: Activity 4

1. I have to be very careful because I'm allergic to all nuts and cannot eat peanut butter.
2. Some foods have hidden nuts, such as cookies and cupcakes.
3. Quebec City is famous for Bonhomme and Winter Carnival.
4. The St. Lawrence River forms a boundary between Canada and the United States.
5. Sentences will vary.

Week 10: Activity 5

1. Students <u>who work hard</u> will be successful on this test. R
2. Kingston, <u>where Marty was born</u>, is becoming a large city. NR
3. Lyle and Lucy, <u>who live next door</u>, have jobs in Toronto. NR
4. The wind, <u>which was strong and cold</u>, gave the hikers frostbite. NR
5. Harry <u>who was very tired</u> kept running until he reached the finish line. R

Bonus Activity: Idioms

b	u	c	k	e	t		b			m	
e		r					i			u	
e		y					l	e	a	s	t
		s					l			i	
		t						n	e	c	k
	l		a	w			f	o	x		
h	o	l	d				l				
				h	e	a	d				
						s	h	e	e	t	
						h					

Week 11: Activity 1

1. Canada has two official languages, French and English.
2. Both languages are taught in many schools throughout Canada.
3. She doesn't lose her temper <u>even when she is really tired</u>.
4. I will help you with your history project <u>if I have time</u>.
5. Go <u>to Stewart St.</u>, turn <u>to the left</u>, follow <u>all the signs</u> and you will find the yard sale.

Week 11: Activity 2

1. Present   2. Past
3. In Kim's garden, she grew tomatoes, beans, radishes, and zucchini.
4. It is great to be able to eat fresh vegetables all summer long.
5. Don't be rude; don't be sassy; don't talk back.

Week 11: Activity 3

1. Each morning, I start the day with a cup of coffee, tea, or hot chocolate.
2. For breakfast, I like hot cereal, toast, fruit, or maybe scrambled eggs.
3. (Papers and cans) <u>littered the yard and made it look messy</u>.
4. (Sarah and her sister) <u>closed their eyes and made a wish</u>.
5. Since you are so <u>flexible</u>, I will help you on Saturday. Willing and able to adapt or change

Week 11: Activity 4

1. Declarative
2. Interrogative
3. My youngest sister, Bella, likes all kinds of ice cream except for strawberry.

4. I need some new shoes, some cleats, and a pair of black flats.
5. Intransitive

Week 11: Activity 5
1. Studying leaves is fascinating because there are so many different kinds.
2. Leaves come in different shades of green and no two kinds are the same.
3. Leaves that grow in shade are often dark green while leaves that grow in sunlight are lighter.
4. A leaf's shape is important because we can tell a lot about a tree from its leaf's shape.
5. Some leaves have complex shapes which lets the wind blow them easily.

Bonus Activity: What to Do?
1. preview   2. deposit   3. grief   4. penalty
5. business   6. magnet

Week 12: Activity 1
1. Sen.
2. Mr. Burtch told us to open our books to the poem, A Ballad of John Silver, by John Masefield.
3. It is the story of John Silver, leader of the pirate gang, in the story Treasure Island.
4. Everyone in my family (worked hard to clean up leaves and plant the garden.)
5. All the fans in the stands (cheered loudly for the home team.)

Week 12: Activity 2
1. When we fly to Edmonton, our dog Scoots, will be staying home at the Paws Inn.
2. It is a pet hotel where animals can stay while their owners are away from home.
3. Dad's research work is (challenging) and (rewarding.)
4. You seem (sad) and (lonely) today.
5. who's   weren't

Week 12: Activity 3
1. My brother didn't have any idea how I was able to find his hiding place in the dark.
2. Dave and Eddie said they're watching the action movie The Return of Zorro tonight.
3. The art summer (program) offers its program to students of all ages.

4. (Jenny) will be showing her best landscapes in their show.
5. signature: 3   appropriate: 4

Week 12: Activity 4
1. Neither Barry nor George passed their history test on the War of 1812.
2. Miss Downes said they could do a makeup test on Friday after school.
3. Exclamatory   4. Declarative   5. Transitive

Week 12: Activity 5
1. "I saw it with my own eyes," said Gerry. "A stretch limo on Main Street!"
2. "I think you are kidding me about that," I answered back quickly.
3. "Who would be coming into our town in a car like that?" asked Bill. "A rock star?"
4. "Maybe it's a scout for a major hockey team," added Toby, "or a basketball team."
5. "Hey guys," shouted Roger, "did you see the limo for my cousin's wedding?"

Bonus Activity: What Does It Mean?
1. implicate   2. pay it out   3. defame   4. deny
5. choice   6. infringe on   7. declare

Week 13: Activity 1
1. We have to finish our homework, whether we want to or not.
2. Mom's homemade soup is a delicious treat for lunch on any day.
3. She puts lots of vegetables, chicken and some spices in it.
4. British Columbia's Rocky Mountains
5. the Browns' ATV

Week 13: Activity 2
1. Because I missed the bus, I was late for class.
2. Synonyms: artificial, unreal, phony, forgery
   Antonyms: genuine, real, authentic, pure
3. Tammy practises her skating every day because she wants to win the competition.
4. Uncle Steve collects old clocks which he buys at flea markets and yard sales.
5. Jenny doesn't

Week 13: Activity 3

1. Mom is the <u>best</u> dancer in her family.
2. Their two dogs barked all night and woke up the whole neighbourhood.
3. We visited the Canadian National Exhibition or CNE while we were in Toronto.
4. rough: roughness, roughage
5. fight: fighter

Week 13: Activity 4

1. Answers will vary.
2. "Todd," Mrs. Greenwood said, "Please explain your answer to the class."
3. By the time we returned from fishing, we were wet, tired and hungry.
4. you   5. they

Week 13: Activity 5

1. Prince Edward Island has a rocky coast which may be dangerous for ships so lighthouses warn ships of the dangers.
2. The Calgary Stampede, which runs for ten days in July has one exciting event called chuck wagon racing.
3. Saskatchewan, a prairie province with very flat land, is famous for the wheat grown there.
4. Many tourists like to visit the Canadian side of Niagara Falls, or Horseshoe Falls, in Ontario.

Bonus Activity: Categories

1. chain   2. hyphen   3. generator   4. almond
5. proverb   6. clause   7. mythology

Week 14: Activity 1

1. In 1967, Canada held a big celebration for its first centennial.
2. In 2017, we will celebrate one hundred fifty years as a nation.
3. The ability to read and write.
4. If your story (is) written, you (may) read it to me.
5. The whole event (is) becoming clearer to me now.

Week 14: Activity 2

1. My cousin is named April Louise which is her grandmother's name too.
2. Playing basketball, running cross-country, and swimming are good exercise.
3. hers   4. theirs
5. 1, 5, 3, 2, 4, 6

Week 14: Activity 3

1. Before noon, we had <u>caught</u> ten fish for our fish fry.
2. He was <u>running</u> five kilometres a day to get in shape.
3. Great-grandpa Don turned 100 on October 10 so we had a big party to celebrate.
4. Sam, our baseball team captain, tries hard to keep our team working their best.
5. An (aide) to the Prime Minister will arrange that meeting.

Week 14: Activity 4

1. My mom's favourite TV show is <u>Chopped</u> and she watches it every week.
2. Once I asked her, "Would you ever like to appear on that show?"
3. The (cat) woke up, stretching <u>its</u> legs.
4. (Selena's) cousins said they would help <u>her</u> sew the costumes.
5. unacceptable

Week 14: Activity 5

1. Foods <u>that are high in sugar</u> are high in calories too. R
2. Children <u>who disobey the rules</u> will lose their privileges. R
3. Our cottage is on an island <u>where everyone knows each other</u>. NR
4. Chocolate <u>which is my favourite flavour</u> is a popular choice of ice cream. NR
5. Sherry <u>who is my best friend</u> won the Artist of the Year Award. NR

Bonus Activity: Analogies

1. Salt is to pepper as bread is to butter.
2. Author is to book as artist is to painting.
3. Research is to researcher as garden is to gardener.
4. Breakfast is to lunch as morning is to noon.
5. TV is to commercial as magazine is to ad.
6. Manager is to store as principal is to school.
7. Chair is to table as mattress is to bed.

Week 15: Activity 1

1. Transitive   2. Intransitive
3. We drove (to the beach) and ate our lunch (at the picnic table.)
4. Because she is so quiet, she never disturbs anyone.

5. "Help me set the table," called Mom, " so we can eat early."

Week 15: Activity 2

1. My (friend), Sasha, is learning how to dive.
2. Please tell the waiter that we don't need any more bread with our meal.
3. He cut his foot on a clam shell at the beach and it bled a lot.
4. formulae   5. pianos

Week 15: Activity 3

1. Grandma's cookies and doughnuts (tasted) delicious.
2. Imperative
3. Declarative
4. Sarah's note said "Meet me at the library after science class."
5. Puffins nest along the Avalon coastline of Newfoundland.

Week 15: Activity 4

1. kg   2. cm
3. An "ice road" is a name given to a river that freezes with ice over a metre thick.
4. They are used as roads during the Arctic winter and they even hold heavy trucks.
5. Jan owns a flourishing business.

Week 15: Activity 5

1. We are going swimming at Crystal Beach with some friends.
2. I like to read good books in a quiet room all by myself.
3. Where is my brand new red sweater that I left in on the couch last night ?
4. Today is a gloomy day and it looks like it is going to rain so it would be a good day for a nap.

Bonus Activity: Story Board

Check story board for details listed in story.

Week 16: Activity 1

1. Putting in time
2. If you arrive early at the party, you can help me set up the tables.
3. When the guest of honour gets here, we will all yell, "Surprise!"
4. If you eat quicker than others, you might get a stomach ache.
5. When Mr. Howard dropped his briefcase, all his papers blew away.

Week 16: Activity 2

1. We won't ask him to help us (unless) we really need him.
2. Transitive   3. Intransitive
4. Whenever you're worried about something, remember to breathe deeply.
5. Charlotte, who is my cousin, is taking a cake decorating class at Parkwood High.

Week 16: Activity 3

1. truthful 2. worthy, worthless
3. The soccer team will play their game (whether) it rains (or) not.
4. Yesterday we found some glasses, a jacket, and a library book on the park bench.
5. We don't know whose they are so we left them at the public library.

Week 16: Activity 4

1. "Would you like toast, cereal, or scrambled eggs for breakfast?" asked Mom.
2. "How about a bacon, lettuce, and tomato sandwich?" I replied.
3. The winning soccer team and their coach (were congratulated after the game.)
4. We (will check tomorrow's newspaper for their picture.)
5. hallucination: 5   prosperous: 3

Week 16: Activity 5

When the first settlers came to Canada, they had to find shelter quickly. Their first homes were log cabins, huts made from mud and bark, or dugouts which were simply caves dug into hillsides. Can you imagine surviving in such harsh conditions? As soon as possible, the settlers worked to replace these temporary homes with more safe, comfortable ones. Most homes were made of wood. Some had wooden shingles but most homes had thatched roofs.

Bonus Activity: Up! Up! And Away! Word Search

B	R	O	K	E	N	S	K	U	L	L			T	
O		I				C						T		
N		D				H		U						
E		R				E	Y	E	B	R	O	W		
	E	H	E	A	R	T	S	L			N	A	I	L
G		Y	F	O	O	T		B						
N				O				N	O	G	G	I	N	
I			E	T				W	A	J				
F			T	H	U	M	B							

Week 17: Activity 1

1. Billy tries to study harder this year for his history tests.
2. He wants to be on the honour roll when he graduates in June.
3. Canada's most important export
4. chocolate cake's ingredients
5. most honest

Week 17: Activity 2

1. Over the <u>hills</u>, and through the <u>woods</u>, to grandmother's <u>house</u>, we go.
2. We spent the day at the <u>beach</u>, playing in the <u>sand</u> and jumping off the <u>dock</u>.
3. "Rudy, can you buy some food for Rover when you go shopping?" asked Dale.
4. "What kind is best for a dog of his size?" replied Rudy.
5. Waiting for their favourite runner to pass by, the <u>fans</u> (cheered) when she came into sight.

Week 17: Activity 3

1. <u>After</u> we finished our homework, we watched TV.
2. Mom was mad <u>because</u> we left our rooms in a mess.
3. should've
4. Rockwood High will play the final game of the season against Johnstown High.
5. All during the game, the crowd was very enthusiastic about the score.

Week 17: Activity 4

1. Capt.   2. Apr.
3. On July 1, 1867, four provinces united to become the Dominion of Canada.
4. Over the next few years, more provinces joined and our country grew in size.
5. meatball is to spaghetti as chocolate chip is to cookie

Week 17: Activity 5

1. Processed food contains a lot of salt so it is not a good idea to eat too much of it.
2. Jan's family used to live in Calgary but they live in Edmonton now.
3. Because deciduous trees lose their leaves every year, it is hard work to clean up all those leaves.
4. Our public library has great books so I borrow books from there all the time.
5. This year I have a new teacher named Ms. Doyle who is a funny person.

Bonus Activity: Fix It

Marianne wanted to acquire a saltwater <u>aquarium</u>. She was worried about the <u>expense</u> and the care it <u>would</u> need. So she did some <u>research</u> so she <u>would</u> know the <u>exact</u> care and time <u>involved</u>. One <u>source</u> said she needed to put the water in the aquarium and wait six weeks before she added the fish. "Good grief! That's <u>too</u> <u>much</u> work," thought Marianne. So she got a puppy from her <u>neighbour</u> <u>instead</u>.

Week 18: Activity 1

1. Fragment   2. Complete sentence
3. We haven't put away all of those groceries so don't look in the cupboard.
4. If you want to help us, we are glad to have one more person.
5. Josie <u>doesn't like</u> getting cold so she <u>will</u> stay inside if the temperature <u>is</u> falling fast.

Week 18: Activity 2

1. Mom hit the garage (door) with her <u>car</u>.
2. I will finish my (homework) on my <u>laptop</u>.
3. "Sit in the same seats while I check your attendance," said Mr. Clark.
4. "Terrific!" he said. "This must be a record. Everyone is present today."
5. organization

Week 18: Activity 3

1. Because everyone in my family likes animals, we have three cats, two dogs, and a rabbit.
2. Everyone helps to feed, water, and sometimes bath each one of our pets.
3. embark   4. adjust
5. If you need help, you <u>should</u> ask your teacher.

Week 18: Activity 4

1. Exclamatory
2. When the little kids play in the sandbox, their shoes get full of dirt.
3. They have lots of fun playing with their pails, shovels, and toy trucks.
4. his   5. theirs

Week 18: Activity 5

1. A voice over the loudspeaker said, "Would Jon Kent please come to the office?"
2. "Who are the candidates for school mayor?" asked the principal.
3. "Candidates need to prepare a speech," said Mrs Owen. "They will speak on Friday."
4. "We need to work together," said Roger, "if we are going to help Annie win."
5. Whose slogan is "Want the best? Vote for Tess"?

Bonus Activity: A Bunch of Groups

1. geese   2. bears   3. elephants   4. ants   5. sheep
6. seals   7. lions

Week 19: Activity 1

1. I saw a moose when I was in Newfoundland with my family in July.
2. It was wandering down the road and it wasn't paying any attention to the traffic.
3. George put his jacket in the closet.
4. ours   5. theirs

Week 19: Activity 2

1. Here are three types of angles to measure in degrees. OR Measure these three angles in degrees.
2. My cousin, Harry, who lives in Windsor, Ontario, doesn't have any brothers or sisters.
3. He likes to visit our farm each summer because we have a big family.
4. You won't be allowed to go until your mother gives you permission.
5. After we go to the movie, we are going to Pizza Palace.

Week 19: Activity 3

1. We visited both the Parliament Buildings and the Royal Canadian Mint.
2. The weather is better today than yesterday.
3. It becomes better each day as summer approaches.
4. In 1894, Margaret Marshall Saunders wrote Beautiful Joe, an autobiography of a dog.
5. It is believed to be the first Canadian book to sell one million copies.

Week 19: Activity 4

1. Imperative   2. Interrogative
3. Put an end to it right away/before it started
4. We don't know whose backpack was found on the bus.
5. We left it in the Lost and Found near the principal's office.

Week 19: Activity 5

15 - mysterious	3 - antique	14 - mansion
12 - investigate	5 - contemporary	16 - reside
19 - solution	7 - electric	4 - bungalow
17 - scarlet	9 - genuine	8 - elegant
13 - ivory	18 - sincere	6 - dowdy
11 - indigo	10 - impostor	20 - wandering
1 - accumulate	2 - acquire	21 - zany

Bonus Activity: In Other Words

1. h   2. a   3. e   4. d   5. g   6. b   7. f   8. c

Week 20: Activity 1

1. Fragment
2. Neither Will nor Wally knew the correct answer to my question.
3. We don't know for sure whether we leave at 7:00 a.m. or 7:30 a.m.
4. Because Jen and I weren't ready for the test, we scored worse than we should have.
5. We are going to ask Ms. Kerr if we are able to rewrite it on Monday.

Week 20: Activity 2

1. "I need to change my clothes," said Mark, "before I go on a hike with you."
2. "Bring your backpack with some snacks, a water bottle, and bug spray," I yelled.
3. You are not going to make the team unless you come to practice each day.
4. While you pick up the toys, I will load the dishwasher.
5. Clean off the table and we will play a board game. you.

Week 20: Activity 3

1. I can't leave yet <u>because</u> my mother is not home from work.
2. Let's buy some new pencils, crayons, and notebooks for school.
3. They have big bargains on school supplies right now at the Best Price and Value store.
4. (Squirrels) like to build <u>their</u> nests high up in trees.
5. The (osprey) laid four eggs in <u>its</u> nest.

Week 20: Activity 4

1. <u>We haven't</u> seen that new movie yet.
2. <u>It 'll</u> soon be in theatres near us.
3. Queen Elizabeth ll, Canada's queen, is the longest reigning monarch in our history.
4. She lives in Buckingham Palace in London, England, with her husband, Prince Phillip.
5. The <u>sun</u> smiled down on the earth below.

Week 20: Activity 5

1. Because I have to get my hair cut, I won't be able to meet you at noon but I will meet you later.
2. My dad likes to read the sports section of the newspaper and Mom likes the gardening news.
3. Peanuts, also called legumes, are related to peas and beans and grow underground.
4. Dr. Greene, our dentist, has a big practice and her office is in Medford.

Bonus Activity: Champlain in the Colonies

1. rich   2. craftsmen   3. settlers   4. large tracts of land

Week 21: Activity 1

1. The (boys) and (girls) were already in <u>their</u> seats.
2. If you spill (chocolate milk) on your shirt, <u>it</u> will leave a stain.
3. That Ferris wheel turns faster than any ride I have ever been on.
4. As my Aunt Celia boarded the bus for Moose Jaw, I waved goodbye sadly.
5. Emma (and) Drew love computer games, (but) Andy doesn't.

Week 21: Activity 2

1. Would you like to live in Paris, Rome, or London in the future?
2. Not me. I would prefer Victoria, Quebec City or Edmonton.
3. squiggly   4. accidental
5. Compound

Week 21: Activity 3

1. more serious, most serious
2. These are your books on the table and those on the shelf are mine.
3. Chloe works at Pizza Palace on Monday and Wednesday nights and on Saturdays.
4. Fragment   5. Complete sentence

Week 21: Activity 4

1. Miss Vogel read the poem <u>The Lady of Shalott</u> by Alfred Lord Tennyson to our class.
2. It is a sad tale about a young woman who escaped her prison on an island.
3. Simple   4. Compound
5. more quietly

Week 21: Activity 5

1. Space is to rocket as <u>water</u> is to boat.
2. Mechanic is to motors as plumber is to <u>pipes</u>.
3. Fame is to famous as study is to <u>studious</u>.
4. Brake is to stop as engine is to <u>go</u>.
5. Page is to book as <u>province</u> is to Canada.

Bonus Activity: Comparing Adjectives

1. quieter, quietest   2. more serious, most serious
3. dreamier, dreamiest   4. classier, classiest
5. slowest   6. poorer   7. thinnest   8. worst   9. finer
10. bigger   11. wider   12. shorter

Week 22: Activity 1

1. By the time Harvey reached home, he had <u>driven</u> 300 kilometres.
2. He has <u>worked</u> in Toronto for three years now.
3. mountaineer: 3
4. This year the weather has been colder in February than in January.
5. People who like winter sports, like skiing and skating, enjoy the cold weather.

Week 22: Activity 2

1. I <u>haven't</u> got <u>no</u> time to wait for you. I have no time or I haven't any time
2. <u>If your tooth is still hurting</u>, call the dentist.
3. He had already left <u>when I returned from the store</u>.
4. "Watch out!" called Jackie. "That step is broken in

two places."

5. "Thanks for warning me." said Anne. "I didn't see anything wrong."

Week 22: Activity 3

1. <u>Although</u> it was carefully planned, the fundraiser was not a success.
2. You will need to study <u>until</u> you know all those multiplication facts.
3. interfering, fertilizer
4. We were going to attend the game but the weather forecaster said it was freezing rain.
5. My dad refuses to drive in bad weather because he says he has no control over the car.

Week 22: Activity 4

1. Some desert areas <u>are</u> cold.
2. Entering the store, Fred walked down the centre aisle to the puzzles' shelf.
3. The car shown on the brochure was an new model Chevrolet.
4. Ragged, unkempt, messy
5. Upset, anxious, hysterical

Week 22: Activity 5

The frankfurter, named for the city of Frankfurt, Germany, is easily the most popular sausage in the world. Frankfurters, more commonly known as hot dogs, are sold almost everywhere in North America. They are a favourite food at sporting events, amusement parks, and fairs. What family barbeque would be complete without hot dogs? You might enjoy one with ketchup, relish, or mustard, or even eat it plain. Do you think other people of the world enjoy hot dogs as much as Canadians do?

Bonus Activity: What's Next?

Answers will vary.

Week 23: Activity 1

1. Gen. Stevens was a commander during World War l in England.
2. Because Marianne and Tina enjoy dance, they go to many performances.
3. You may chose <u>either</u> to go to the movies <u>or</u> have a sleepover for your birthday.
4. The (salmon) swims upstream to lay <u>its</u> eggs.
5. (Jack) cleaned <u>his</u> room and closet too.

Week 23: Activity 2

1. In a unanimous vote, Lizzy was declared the new class president.
2. My neighbours, Vicki and Ross, are moving to Cold Lake, Alberta, in October.
3. <u>A perfect, shiny, red apple</u> grew near the top of the tree.
4. <u>Todd</u> climbed the ladder so he could pick it.
5. nonviolent

Week 23: Activity 3

1. "Look out!" called Pete. "The wagon of wood is tipping over!"
2. Joe didn't feel very well after he ate four hotdogs and drank two drinks.
3. Hugh said he was walking to school alone, <u>so we left without him</u>.
4. The ceremony was <u>simple</u> and <u>tasteful</u>.
5. The soft snow looked <u>fluffy</u> and <u>light</u>.

Week 23: Activity 4

1. I don't know where mom and dad <u>have</u> gone.
2. future
3. My dad <u>hiked</u> there when he was my age. past
4. On May 21, 2013, my Aunt Bonnie graduated from Dalhousie University.
5. We had an celebration and everyone wished her all the best in her new career.

Week 23: Activity 5

1. Imperative   2. Exclamatory   3. Interrogative
4. Declarative   5. Imperative

Bonus Activity: Gender Nouns Crossword

w			g			q	u	e	e	n
a	c	t	o	r						
i			d				e			
t			d		g		m	a	n	
r		h	e	i	r		p			
e			s		a		r			
s			s		n	i	e	c	e	
s					d		s		b	
					s	i	s	t	e	r
					o				i	
				u	n	c	l	e		
									d	
									e	

Week 24: Activity 1

1. mine
2. Our class is creating a play based on O. Henry's <u>The Ransom of Red Chief</u>.
3. It is a humorous story about a badly behaved boy and two simple fellows.
4. irregular   5. unknown

Week 24: Activity 2

1. Simple   2. Compound
3. Our volunteers will work all day Saturday to clean up the playground at Hyde Park.
4. We will be cutting the grass, picking up trash, fixing the swings and painting the benches.
5. Exclamatory

Week 24: Activity 3

1. fragment
2. We're going to upgrade our computer so it's faster.
3. We are going shopping on Friday at Computer World on Brock Street.
4. Grandma put the (flowers) in a beautiful vase.
5. She picked (asters) and (daisies) from her own garden.

Week 24: Activity 4

1. "Yes, Annie," said Mom, "I made chocolate cake for tonight's dessert."
2. "Did you put chocolate or vanilla icing on it? I asked.
3. The weather <u>becomes</u> cooler in September and October.
4. After that we <u>can</u> expect the snow to start falling.
5. address: addresses   goalie: goalies

Week 24: Activity 5

1. Make someone feel comfortable; offer friendship
2. Work extra hard
3. By a very small margin
4. A loud, jolly laugh
5. A severe scolding; reprimand

Bonus Activity: Natural Resources

*1.   2. e   *3. d   4. c   *5. f   *6. a

Week 25: Activity 1

1. "When a liquid is heated, it releases vapours," explained Mr. Clark.
2. "Many liquids," he continued, "turn to a solid when they are cooled."
3. <u>Delicious, cinnamon</u> (smells) filled the air,
4. <u>Our talented</u> (sister) cooks many treats for us.
5. We heard the noise <u>of</u> the branches falling <u>on</u> the roof <u>of</u> our house.

Week 25: Activity 2

1. During this month, I need to go to my mother's office after school.
2. My dad is tied up with business meetings and isn't home very early at night.
3. decision: decide   gangster: gang
4. Maniwaki: 4   5. Wabakimi: 4

Week 25: Activity 3

1. We are <u>planning</u> a big family dinner for Thanksgiving.
2. Relatives are <u>coming</u> from far away for the event.
3. "I just saw the cutest little puppies at Sam's Pet Shop," exclaimed Fiona.
4. "I think I am going to ask my parents if they would consider letting me get one," she added.
5. the sharp claws belonging to the cat : the cat's sharp claws

Week 25: Activity 4

1. All the Grade 7 lockers are on the first floor in the hall next to the gym.
2. Try to keep your locker neat so you are able to find your books quickly.
3. music
4. When my friend Yan came to Canada, <u>she couldn't speak any English</u>.
5. <u>She tried hard each day</u> so she could learn more words.

Week 25: Activity 5

1. Ms Blair, our math teacher, she gives us lots of homework every night.
2. I looked for Jake at the movie but he wasn't there because he had stayed home instead.
3. Dawn and Audrey are spending the weekend in Montreal and they are visiting their cousins.
4. <u>Island</u> is the story of ship carrying young teens, who are troubled kids who need help.
5. At my sleepover on Saturday night, we will have pizza and chips.

BONUS ACTIVITY: SAINT-PIERRE AND MIGUELON

1. T   2. F   3. F

WEEK 26: ACTIVITY 1

1. A superhuman helper
2. Very easy to understand
3. Maggie and Pete are learning how to skateboard at the Hawkins Youth Centre.
4. A team of skateboarders is teaching them how to be safe and have fun too.
5. (Polly and Hector) went to the museum with their class.

WEEK 26: ACTIVITY 2

1. prefix: disallow   suffix: allows, allowing, allowed, allowance
2. prefix: dislike   suffix: likes, liked, liking, likable, likely
3. Janice wrote a human interest (story) for the local newspaper.
4. "Wow! Look at those awesome basketball shoes," exclaimed Franco.
5. "I haven't got enough money for those shoes," I replied.

WEEK 26: ACTIVITY 3

1. If you have looked everywhere for your jacket, then it must be lost.
2. You will have some dessert when you have eaten you vegetables.
3. That book is a good story about an adventure on a ship.
4. I like adventure and mystery stories best especially if the are true.
5. Past

WEEK 26: ACTIVITY 4

1. If you're hungry after school, have some yogurt, celery, or popcorn to eat.
2. Eric Wilson, author of many Canadian novels, likes to visit classrooms.
3. She broke her arm when she fell off her bicycle.
4. Because her arm needed to heal, she had a cast on it.
5. When the game ends, everyone claps and cheers.

WEEK 26: ACTIVITY 5

1. subject: judge   predicate: awarded
2. subject: castle   predicate: looked
3. subject: conservation   predicate: receives
4. subject: family   predicate: is buying
5. subject: rain   predicate: fell

BONUS ACTIVITY: I WILL FOLLOW YOU ....

1. belong to   2. hint at / about   3. scoff at   4. refer to
5. listen to   6. lead into   7. stare at   8. side with
9. sympathize with   10. consist of   11. depend on / upon   12. glance at / over   13. agree with   14. laugh at / about

WEEK 27: ACTIVITY 1

1. "Open your mouth and say 'Ah', " said the dentist.
2. You have two cavities that need to be filled as soon as possible.
3. After you set the table, call your brother to come in.
4. We will eat as soon as your mother gets home from work.
5. Imperative

WEEK 27: ACTIVITY 2

1. In autumn, leaves turn red, yellow, orange and brown.
2. The bread smelled garlicky and delicious.
3. 4, 2, 3, 5, 6, 1
4. We need to find some information about Canada's lumbering industry.
5. Don't you know the best places to look for facts about this topic?

WEEK 27: ACTIVITY 3

1. Very pleased; rewarded   2. A pest
3. "We have a wonderful surprise today," Ms Southern told her kindergarten class.
4. "Sparky the Fire Safety Dog is coming to visit us and tell us how to be safe."
5. Because we won, our coach bought everyone (pizza and soft drinks.)

WEEK 27: ACTIVITY 4

1. Be brave; don't cry or whine
2. Nobody is sure what happened to Tom's bike which he left outside last night.
3. After their day-long nap, the cats ran up and down the stairs all night.
4. Complex   5. Compound

WEEK 27: ACTIVITY 5

Present: today, presently, now, currently
Past: yesterday, recently, before, earlier
Future: later, tomorrow, next, after

Bonus Activity: Give Me a "C"

c	h	i	l	l	i	w	a	c	k		c
a	c	l	l	a	w	n	r	o	c	c	h
m	a		u	a	e	l	p	a	h	c	a
b	l				a		a	u	c		m
r	g			g		t	c	r	a	p	
i	a		n		h	a		c	m	l	
d	r	o		a	n			h	r	a	
g	y	b	m	s				i	o	i	
e	a		o					l	s	n	
c	l	a	r	e	n	v	i	l	l	e	

Week 28: Activity 1

1. worst   2. patiently
3. The Bronson family built a new house on the corner of Archer Street and Bay Street.
4. "Hey, I'd like to join in that game you are playing," said Mark.
5. ptarmigan: 3   whippoorwill: 3

Week 28: Activity 2

1. Complete sentence
2. The little boy screamed, "I want my mommy right now!"
3. "Does anyone have an idea for our science project?" asked Terri.
4. Henry's sports car is small but powerful.
5. Your stories are funny, unusual and entertaining.

Week 28: Activity 3

1. The sock with the (hole) belongs to my (brother.)
2. We sat at a picnic (table) in the peaceful (park.)
3. The scenes in that movie were gruesome but the sound effects were even more horrible. 122
4. The Bailey kids want a puppy but their parents aren't so sure about the idea.
5. Chloe, our next door neighbour, is playing soccer in the Greenville Girls League.

Week 28: Activity 4

1. boss: bosses   wax: waxes
2. Peggy, our cousin from Moose Jaw, lost weight because she started running.
3. Historians believe that the Vikings were the first visitors to Canada.
4. M   5. F

Week 28: Activity 5

1. Sunglasses were invented many years ago by the Inuit. The Inuit invented sunglasses many years ago.
2. A pair made from walrus ivory was found by hunters in Baffin, Quebec. Hunters in Baffin, Quebec, found a pair made from walrus ivory.
3. A tiny slit was cut in the bone or antlers by carvers to make the sunglasses. Carvers cut a tiny slit in the bone to make the sunglasses.
4. These sunglasses were used by the Inuit to protect against snow blindness. The Inuit used these sunglasses to protect against snow blindness.
5. The sunglasses can be seen by visitors to the Canadian Museum of Civilization. Visitors to the Canadian Museum of Civilization can see the sunglasses.

Bonus Activity: I'm So Confused ?????

1. I should have heeded his advice and stayed out of trouble.
2. They will sow the seeds when the weather warms up.
3. The 12 children will share the snacks among them.
4. We all laughed at the sight of him in the funny costume.
5. Please raise your hand before you speak.
6. He didn't seem to realize how that would affect him.
7. They did not intend to alter the original plan.

Week 29: Activity 1

1. Visitors to Quebec City like to photograph the many old historic buildings.
2. We need to finish our homework, take a shower, and wash our hair.
3. kingdom   4. amusement
5. The rabbit in the cage was twitching its nose.

Week 29: Activity 2

1. Canada has the largest colony of Atlantic puffins in North America.
2. It is found in Newfoundland's Witless Bay Ecological Reserve.
3. We will soon have to wean the puppies from their mother. Feed them from a dish
4. They will use a bulldozer to excavate a big hole. dig
5. synonyms

Week 29: Activity 3

1. "These cookies looks delicious but are they peanut-free?" asked Ali.

2. Molly's first visit to Winnipeg was on July 1, 2006, when she was six years old.
3. The music coming from his bedroom was too loud.
4. I got up early so the day <u>seemed</u> longer than usual.
5. She is learning to skate. <u>But not very well right now.</u> fragment

Week 29: Activity 4

1. People in the <u>news</u> are often embarrassed by the <u>reports</u> of the <u>press</u>.
2. The drugstore in our <u>town</u> is open for <u>business</u> for six <u>days</u> of the <u>week</u>.
3. We are going to Landon Bay to join a conservation program called Local Wildlife.
4. They will teach all about how to protect animals, native plants, and birds.
5. <u>Oh no!</u> This is terrible!

Week 29: Activity 5

1. <u>As the last of the guests left</u>, she gave a sigh of relief.
2. <u>If you do not follow the rules</u>, you may be in trouble.
3. Good friends are helpers (in time of trouble.)
4. (In the last few minutes,) our team won the game.
5. The crowd cheered <u>as the monkey performed his tricks.</u>

Bonus Activity: Where Do I Look?

1. dictionary   2. cookbook   3. thesaurus   4. atlas
5. thesaurus

Week 30: Activity 1

1. Our town (is) building a new library and the community (is) donating books for it.
2. Even though I heard that story before, I still listened for the surprise ending.
3. "Would you like to read a story by the same author?" asked the librarian.
4. Jeff gave <u>me</u> a free (ticket) to his hockey game tonight.
5. The book won <u>her</u> instant (fame).

Week 30: Activity 2

1. intransitive
2. On a beautiful autumn day, I like to stroll through the woods and collect leaves.
3. Sometimes I put them in books to press them so I can make a display.
4. hers   5. hers

Week 30: Activity 3

1. <u>Max and Ruby</u> is a popular TV show for young children and it is on every day.
2. I prefer to watch nature shows like <u>Wild Kingdom</u> or <u>Strange and Unusual Animals</u>.
3. The old friends sat <u>under the shady tree</u> and visited.
4. Our new principal seems <u>strict</u> but <u>fair</u>.
5. She is <u>popular</u> with all the students.

Week 30: Activity 4

1. Sun block is important to remember to bring to the beach.
2. Bring some sandwiches, fruit, pickles, and drinks and we'll have a picnic.
3. happy
4. Declarative   5. Interrogative

Week 30: Activity 5: Pronoun or Adjective?

1. Adjective   2. Pronoun   3. Pronoun   4. Pronoun
5. Adjective

Bonus Activity: Categories

Units of Money: nickel; loonie; dime; quarter; toonie; cheque
Place to keep $$$: wallet; bank account; cash register; safe; bank; vault
Foreign Money: peso; franc; ruble; shilling; lira; yen
What We Do with $$$: pay; invest; collet; save; earn; spend

Week 31: Activity 1

1. We will understand the lives of early people (if) we study their history.
2. Toronto, (which) is a large city, is a commercial, cultural and communications centre.
3. Mavis collects old stamps and she has many from Asian countries.
4. Sometimes she finds old stamps at yard sales or at auctions.
5. Intransitive

Week 31: Activity 2

1. The wind created some (cooling) breezes for the runners.
2. We knew he was scared from his (shaking) knees.
3. Josie, don't lose your ticket to the concert or you

won't be able to go.
4. "Tomorrow is Pitch In Day," said Mr. Grove, "so come dressed in old clothes."
5. switches, mosquitoes

Week 31: Activity 3

1. Because she has allergies, <u>Allison can't have pets.</u>
2. <u>Our team is going to the tournament</u> if we win the next game.
3. Pause the movie so I can get some snacks. you
4. Nova Scotia, on Canada's Atlantic coast, has the highest tides in the world.
5. Peggy's Cove is visited by thousands of tourists each year.

Week 31: Activity 4

1. The tomatoes in my garden are <u>round, juicy</u> and <u>delicious</u>.
2. <u>The Beaver</u>, our local newspaper, ran an article on solar power.
3. Some people are installing solar panels on their property to produce electricity.
4. All the monarch butterflies (have) flown south.
5. In the spring, they (will) return.

Week 31: Activity 5

1. The ice was cleaned by the zamboni. The zamboni cleaned the ice.
2. The rookie player was honoured by the team. The team honoured the rookie player.
3. Much enjoyment has been given by their performance. Their performance gave much enjoyment.
4. We were told the news of the fire by our neighbours. Our neighbours told us the news of the fire.
5. Paul was presented with the Volunteer of the Year Award by the committee. The committee presented Paul with the Volunteer of the Year Award.

Bonus Activity: Order! Order!

7, 4, 1, 3, 2, 5, 6,

Week 32: Activity 1

1. Many First Nations Canadians lived a harsh life in early times.
2. They survived by hunting, fishing, and growing their own food.
3. windier
4. Subject pronoun   5. Object pronoun

Week 32: Activity 2

1. Simple
2. "Ms Redford, I have to leave class early and go to meet my mom," I said.
3. "That's fine," Ms Redford replied. "Watch the clock and leave when you need to go."
4. <u>Either</u> Dodi or Penny will wash the dishes tonight. Coordinating
5. <u>Although</u> she is tired, my sister will help me with my homework. Subordinating

Week 32: Activity 3

1. that   2. than
3. Since they are grounded, Wally and Jim won't do anything to upset their parents.
4. <u>A Wrinkle in Time</u> is a favourite story of mine to read.
5. (The boys and girls) <u>will sing and dance</u> at the talent show.

Week 32: Activity 4

1. Her parents gave <u>Janet</u> a (kitten) for her birthday.
2. When Mrs. Cook was sick, we helped with the cleaning.
3. She appreciated the kindness of her neighbours.
4. The children dreamed of riding downhill <u>while the snow fell outside.</u>
5. <u>After you finish your work,</u> you may have a treat.

Week 32: Activity 5

1. Finish writing your test, check for errors and hand it in.
2. Our house was damaged by the windstorm when a tree fell on our deck.
3. Sally made delicious cookies yesterday and we ate them all.
4. Joe is a stamp collector who trades with his friends and buys some stamps at sales.
5. We will start soon so you need to be ready with a sharp pencil and a ruler.

Bonus Activity: A Not–So–Secret Message!

Proud to live in a great country

www.ingramcontent.com/pod-product-compliance
Lightning Source LLC
Chambersburg PA
CBHW081204240426
43669CB00039B/2801